The Supporters Guide

to

Premier &

Football League

Clubs

2013

EDITOR
John Robinson

Twenty-ninth Edition

CONTENTS

British Library Cataloguing in Publication Data
A catalogue record for this book is available from the British Library

ISBN: 978-1-86223-238-9

Copyright © 2012, SOCCER BOOKS LIMITED (01472 696226)
72 St. Peter's Avenue, Cleethorpes, N.E. Lincolnshire, DN35 8HU, England
Web site   www.soccer-books.co.uk
e-mail   info@soccer-books.co.uk

Manufactured in the UK by T.J. International Ltd, Padstow

FOREWORD

We are indebted to the staffs of all the clubs featured in this guide for their cooperation and also to Michael Robinson (page layouts), Bob Budd (cover artwork), Tony Brown (Cup Statistics – www.soccerdata.com) and Jim Brailsford for providing photographs of Rotherham United's new stadium.

When using this guide, please note that 'child' concessions also include senior citizens unless stated otherwise. Some clubs (particularly those which were promoted at the end of the 2011-2012 season) had not fixed their matchday admission prices for 2012/2013 at the time of going to press and in these cases we have had to use the 2011/2012 prices in the absence of new information. It should be noted that although actual matchday admission prices are shown in this guide, prices can vary and although many clubs offer discounts for tickets purchased before the day of the game, some prices may be higher than those stated.

Disabled Supporters' information is once again included in the guide and, to ensure that facilities are not overstretched, we recommend that disabled fans pre-book wherever possible.

Regular purchasers of the guide will notice that we have included a number of new ground photographs in this edition. Ground moves and redevelopment are continuing apace and travelling fans may find that away sections and prices change during the course of the 2012/2013 season.

If any readers have alternative ground photos which they would like us to consider for insertion in future issues, they should write to me care of the address opposite.

Finally, we would like to wish our readers a happy and safe spectating season.

John Robinson
EDITOR

WEMBLEY STADIUM

First Opened: 1923 (Re-opened in 2007 after rebuild)
Address: Wembley National Stadium, Wembley,
London   HA9 0WS
Correspondence: P.O.Box 1966, London, SW1P 3EQ
Telephone Nº: 0844 980-8001
Fax Number: (020) 8795-5050

Seating Capacity: 90,000 over three tiers –
  Lower Tier: 34,303 seats
  Middle Tier: 16,532 seats
  Upper Tier: 39,165 seats
Web site: www.wembleystadium.com

GENERAL INFORMATION

Car Parking: The stadium is a Public Transport Location and, as such, parking is only available for pre-accredited vehicles. Any spaces which are available must be pre-purchased from the following web site: www.csparking.com/stadium
Coach Travel: National Express operates 13 coach routes from 43 major towns and cities direct to the stadium for special events: www.nationalexpress.com/wembley
Rail & Tube Travel: Wembley Park station is on the Jubilee and Metropolitan tube lines; Wembley Stadium station is on the Bakerloo tube line and the Silver Link train line; Wembley Central station is on the Chiltern train line which runs from Marylebone Station
Local Bus Services: Services 18, 83, 92, 182 and 224 all travel to the stadium

DISABLED INFORMATION

Wheelchairs: 310 spaces for wheelchairs are available in total alongside 310 seats for helpers. A further 100 enhanced amenity seats are available for ambulant disabled visitors.
Disabled Toilets: Disabled toilets are available throughout the stadium.

ACCRINGTON STANLEY FC

Founded: 1876 (Reformed 1968)
Former Names: None
Nickname: 'Stanley' 'Reds'
Ground: The Crown Ground, Livingstone Road, Accrington, Lancashire BB5 5BX
Record Attendance: 4,368 (3rd January 2004)
Pitch Size: 112 × 72 yards

Colours: Red shirts and shorts
Telephone Nº: (01254) 356950
Fax Number: (01254) 356951
Ground Capacity: 5,070
Seating Capacity: 2,000
Web site: www.accringtonstanley.co.uk
E-mail: info@accringtonstanley.co.uk

GENERAL INFORMATION

Car Parking: Street parking only
Coach Parking: Livingstone Road near the Away entrance
Nearest Railway Station: Accrington (1 mile)
Nearest Bus Station: Accrington Town Centre (1 mile)
Club Shop: At the ground, at Oswaldtwistle Mills Shopping Village and also through the club web site
Opening Times: Weekdays 9.00am – 5.00pm; Saturday matchdays 10.00am – 5.00pm
Telephone Nº: (01254) 356950

GROUND INFORMATION

Away Supporters' Entrances & Sections:
Signposted on matchdays

ADMISSION INFO (2012/2013 PRICES)

Adult Standing: £17.00
Adult Seating: £17.00
Senior Citizen Standing: £12.00
Senior Citizen Seating: £12.00
Ages 12-16 Standing: £7.00
Ages 12-16 Seating: £7.00
Under-12s Standing/Seating: £2.00
Programme Price: £3.00

DISABLED INFORMATION

Wheelchairs: Specific areas around the ground
Helpers: Admitted
Prices: Concessionary prices are charged for the disabled. Helpers are admitted free of charge
Disabled Toilets: Available
Contact: (01254) 356950   Mark Turner, Disabled Liaison Officer (Bookings are necessary)

Travelling Supporters' Information:
Routes: Take the M6 to the M65 signposted for Blackburn/Burnley. Exit at Junction 7 and follow the sign for Padiham. Turn right at first traffic lights then right at next. Follow Whalley Road towards Accrington, go through lights at the Greyhound Inn. Turn left into Livingstone Road, 500 yards past traffic lights (signposted Accrington Stanley). The ground is signposted from Junction 7 of the M65 – follow the brown signs with the white football.

AFC BOURNEMOUTH

Founded: 1899 (**Entered League**: 1923)
Former Names: Boscombe FC (1899-1923);
Bournemouth & Boscombe Athletic FC (1923-1972)
Nickname: 'Cherries'
Ground: Dean Court, Bournemouth, Dorset BH7 7AF
Ground Capacity: 9,776 (All seats)
Record Attendance: 9,762 (22nd January 2011)

Pitch Size: 115 × 74 yards
Colours: Red & Black shirts with Black shorts
Telephone Nº: (01202) 726300
Ticket Office: (01202) 726338
Fax Number: (01202) 726373
Web Site: www.afcb.co.uk
E-mail: enquiries@afcb.co.uk

GENERAL INFORMATION

Car Parking: Car Park for 600 cars behind the ground
Coach Parking: At the ground
Nearest Railway Station: Bournemouth Central (1½ miles)
Nearest Bus Stop: Holdenhurst Road, Bournemouth
Club Shop: At the ground
Opening Times: Monday to Friday 9.00am to 5.00pm and
Saturday Matchdays from 9.00am to kick-off
Telephone Nº: (01202) 726325

GROUND INFORMATION

Away Supporters' Entrances & Sections:
East Stand turnstiles 'F' 14-16 for East Stand accommodation
(Away ticket office is adjacent)

ADMISSION INFO (2012/2013 PRICES)

Adult Seating: £18.00 – £33.00
Child Seating: £5.00 – £15.00
Concessionary Seating: £10.00 – £22.00
Note: Family tickets are also available
Programme Price: £3.00

DISABLED INFORMATION

Wheelchairs: Spaces available in all stands
Helpers: One helper admitted per disabled fan
Prices: Free of charge for both the disabled and helpers
Disabled Toilets: Available in all Stands
Contact: (07803) 090047 (Bookings are necessary)

Travelling Supporters' Information: Routes: From the North & East: Take the A338 into Bournemouth and turn left at 'Kings Park' turning. After the slip road go straight forward at the mini-roundabout into Kings Park Drive – a car park is 500 yards on the left and the ground is nearby; From the West: Head into Bournemouth and join the A338, take the slip road at the Springbourne Roundabout, signposted for Kings Park. Take the 3rd exit at the roundabout at the fire station, stay in the left-hand lane and turn left onto Holdenhurst Road. Go straight on at the traffic lights (the Queen's Park Pub should be on the right) and take the 3rd exit at the mini roundabout into Kings Park for the ground.

AFC WIMBLEDON

Founded: 2002 (**Entered League**: 2011)
Former Names: Originally formed as Wimbledon Old Centrals (1889-1905) who later became Wimbledon FC
Nickname: 'The Dons'
Ground: The Cherry Red Records Fans' Stadium – Kingsmeadow, Jack Goodchild Way, 422A Kingston Road, Kingston-upon-Thames, Surrey   KT1 3PB
Record Attendance: 4,722 (2009)

Pitch Size: 115 × 80 yards
Ground Capacity: 4,700
Seating Capacity: 1,500
Colours: Shirts and Shorts are Blue with Yellow trim
Telephone Nº: (020) 8547-3528
Fax Number: 0808 280-0816
Web site: www.afcwimbledon.co.uk
E-mail: info@afcwimbledon.co.uk

GENERAL INFORMATION

Car Parking: At the ground
Coach Parking: At the ground
Nearest Railway Station: Norbiton (1 mile)
Nearest Bus Station: Kingston
Club Shop: At the ground
Opening Times: Matchdays only
Telephone Nº: (020) 8547-3528

GROUND INFORMATION

Away Supporters' Entrances & Sections:
No usual segregation

ADMISSION INFO (2011/2012 PRICES)

Adult Standing: £15.00
Adult Seating: £17.00 – £19.00
Concessionary Standing: £9.00
Concessionary Seating: £10.00 – £11.00
Under-16s Standing: £2.00
Under-16s Seating: £6.00 – £7.00
Programme Price: £2.50

DISABLED INFORMATION

Wheelchairs: Accommodated around the ground
Helpers: Please phone the club for information
Prices: Please phone the club for information
Disabled Toilets: Yes
Contact: (020) 8547-3528   (Bookings are necessary)

Travelling Supporters' Information:
Routes: Exit the M25 at Junction 10 and take the A3 to the New Malden/Worcester Park turn-off and turn into Malden Road (A2043). Follow Malden Road to the mini-roundabout and turn left into Kingston Road. Kingsmeadow is situated approximately 1 mile up the Kingston Road, on the left-hand side and is signposted from the mini-roundabout.

ALDERSHOT TOWN FC

Founded: 1992   (**Entered League**: 2008)
Former Names: Aldershot FC
Nickname: 'Shots'
Ground: EBB Stadium, Recreation Ground,
High Street, Aldershot   GU11 1TW
Record Attendance: 7,500 (18th November 2000)
Pitch Size: 117 × 76 yards

Colours: Red shirts with Blue trim, Red shorts
Telephone Nº: (01252) 320211
Fax Number: (01252) 324347
Club Secretary: (01252) 320211– Graham Hortop
Ground Capacity: 7,100
Seating Capacity: 1,879
Web site: www.theshots.co.uk
E-mail: enquiries@theshots.co.uk

GENERAL INFORMATION
Supporters Club: c/o Club
Telephone Nº: (01252) 320211
Car Parking: Municipal Car Park is adjacent
Coach Parking: Contact the club for information
Nearest Railway Station: Aldershot (5 mins. walk)
Nearest Bus Station: Aldershot (5 minutes walk)
Club Shop: At the ground
Opening Times: Matchdays only
Telephone Nº: (01252) 320211

GROUND INFORMATION
Away Supporters' Entrances & Sections:
Accommodation in the East Bank Terrace, Bill Warren section
(South Stand) – Redan Hill Turnstiles Nº 11 and 12.

ADMISSION INFO (2012/2013 PRICES)
Adult Standing: £17.00
Adult Seating: £19.00
Under-16s Standing: £5.00 (Under-6s admitted free)
Under-16s Seating: £7.00
Concessionary Standing: £13.00
Concessionary Seating: £15.00
Note: Military personnel are charged Concessionary prices
Programme Price: £3.00

DISABLED INFORMATION
Wheelchairs: Accommodated in the North Stand
Helpers: Admitted
Prices: £13.00 for the disabled, free of charge for helpers
Disabled Toilets: Available
Contact: (01252) 320211   (Bookings are helpful)

Travelling Supporters' Information:
Routes: From the M3: Exit at Junction 4 and follow signs for Aldershot (A331). Leave the A331 at the A323 exit (Ash Road) and continue along into the High Street. The ground is just past the Railway Bridge on the right; From the A31: Continue along the A31 to the junction with the A331, then as above; From the A325 (Farnborough Road): Follow signs to the A323 then turn left into Wellington Avenue. The ground is just off the 2nd roundabout on the left – the floodlights are clearly visible.

ARSENAL FC

Founded: 1886 (**Entered League**: 1893)
Former Names: Royal Arsenal (1886-1891) and
Woolwich Arsenal (1891-1914)
Nickname: 'Gunners'
Ground: Emirates Stadium, Drayton Park   N5
Ground Capacity: 60,335 (All seats)
Pitch Size: 110 × 71 yards
Record Attendance: 60,161 (3rd November 2007)

Colours: Red shirts with White sleeves, White shorts
Telephone Nº: (020) 7619-5000
Ticket Office: 0844 277-3625
Fax Number: (020) 7704-4041
Web Site: www.arsenal.com
E-mail: ask@arsenal.co.uk

GENERAL INFORMATION
Car Parking: None
Coach Parking: Visit the web site for further details
Nearest Railway Station: Finsbury Park and Highbury &
Islington
Nearest Tube Station: Arsenal (Piccadilly), Finsbury Park,
Highbury & Islington and Holloway Road are all nearby
Club Shop: At the ground and at Finsbury Park Tube Station
Opening Times: Monday to Saturday 9.00am to 5.00pm;
Sundays 10.00am to 4.00pm
Telephone Nº: (020) 7619-5000

GROUND INFORMATION
Away Supporters' Entrances & Sections:
Green quadrant – follow colour coding system at the ground

ADMISSION INFO (2012/2013 PRICES)
Adult Seating: £35.00 – £100.00
Child Seating: £14.00 – £25.00 (In the Family Enclosure)
Senior Citizen Seating: £15.00 – £27.00 (Only in the
Family Enclosure)
Note: Prices vary depending on the category of the game.
Programme Price: £3.00

DISABLED INFORMATION
Wheelchairs: 250 spaces available in areas throughout the
ground. A similar number of places are available for the
ambulant disabled and visually impaired
Helpers: One helper admitted for each disabled supporter
Prices: Registered disabled supporters are admitted for half
the normal prices £16.50 – £47.00. Helpers are admitted free
Disabled Toilets: Many available throughout the ground
Free commentaries are available for the visually impaired
Contact: (020) 7619-5050   (Bookings are necessary)

Travelling Supporters' Information:
As the stadium is situated in a mainly residential area, only car owners with resident's permits will be allowed to park in the
designated on-street parking areas. Cars parked illegally will be towed away so use public transport whenever possible. The
nearest tube station is Arsenal (Piccadilly Line) which is 3 minutes walk from the ground with Finsbury Park (Victoria &
Piccadilly Lines) and Highbury & Islington about 10 minutes walk away.

ASTON VILLA FC

Photo courtesy of Neville Williams/Aston Villa FC

Founded: 1874 (**Entered League**: 1888)
Former Names: None
Nicknames: 'The Villans' 'Villa'
Ground: Villa Park, Trinity Road, Birmingham B6 6HE
Ground Capacity: 42,786 (All seats)
Record Attendance: 76,588 (2nd March 1946)
Pitch Size: 115 × 75 yards

Colours: Claret shirts with Blue sleeves, White shorts
Telephone Nº: (0121) 327-2299
Fax Number: (0121) 322-2107
Consumer Sales: 0800 612-0970
Consumer Sales Fax Number: 0800 612-0977
Web Site: www.avfc.co.uk

GENERAL INFORMATION

Ground Tours: 0800 612-0970
Car Parking: Aston Villa Events Centre Car Park in Aston Hall Road.
Away Coach Parking: Opposite the ground on Witton Lane
Nearest Railway Station: Witton or Aston (5 mins. walk)
Nearest Bus Station: Birmingham Centre
Club Shop: 'Villa Village' at the ground + also at New Street in Birmingham City Centre
Opening Times: Monday to Saturday 9.00am to 5.00pm, Sundays 10.00am to 2.00pm, Sunday Matchdays 4 hours before kick-off and 1 hour after the final whistle. City Centre shop open 9.30am to 6.00pm Monday to Saturday, 11.00am to 3.00pm on Sundays.
Telephone Nº: (0121) 326-1559

GROUND INFORMATION

Away Supporters' Entrances & Sections:
Doug Ellis Stand – Blocks 'P' & 'Q'

ADMISSION INFO (2012/2013 PRICES)

Adult Seating: £21.00 – £47.00
Under-16s Seating: £17.00 – £47.00
Senior Citizen Seating: £19.00 – £47.00
Under-22s/Student/Armed Forces: £18.00 – £47.00
Note: Prices vary depending on the category of the game and the location in the stadium
Programme Price: £3.00

DISABLED INFORMATION

Wheelchairs: 84 spaces in total in the Trinity Road Stand lower, 8 of which are for away supporters
Helpers: Admitted on request – one per disabled fan
Prices: £21.00 – £47.00 for disabled fans
Disabled Toilets: Available in the Trinity Road Stand lower
Contact: 0800 612-0970 ext. 344 (Bookings are necessary)
E-mail contact: disability@avfc.co.uk

Travelling Supporters' Information: From all parts: Exit M6 at Junction 6 (Spaghetti Junction). Follow signs for Birmingham (NE). Take the 4th exit at the roundabout onto the A38 (M) signposted Aston. After ½ mile, turn right into Aston Hall Road.
Bus Services: Service 7 from Colmore Circus to Witton Square. Also some specials.

BARNET FC

Founded: 1888
Former Names: Barnet Alston FC
Nickname: 'The Bees'
Ground: Underhill Stadium, Barnet Lane, Barnet, Herts. EN5 2DN
Record Attendance: 11,026 (1952)
Pitch Size: 110 × 70 yards

Colours: Shirts and shorts are Black with Amber Trim
Telephone Nº: (020) 8441-6932
Ticket Office: (020) 8449-6325
Fax Number: (020) 8447-0655
Ground Capacity: 5,567
Seating Capacity: 2,200 approximately
Web site: www.barnetfc.com
E-mail: info@barnetfc.com

GENERAL INFORMATION

Car Parking: Street Parking and High Barnet Underground Car Park
Coach Parking: By Police Direction
Nearest Railway Station: New Barnet (1½ miles)
Nearest Tube Station: High Barnet (Northern) (5 minutes walk)
Club Shop: Located at the South End of the ground
Opening Times: Monday to Friday 9.30am to 5.30pm and Saturday Matchdays from 11.00am to 5.30pm
Telephone Nº: (020) 8441-6932

GROUND INFORMATION

Away Supporters' Entrances & Sections:
Entrances in Westcombe Drive for the North East Terrace and seating areas

ADMISSION INFO (2012/2013 PRICES)

Adult Standing: £14.00 – £17.00
Adult Seating: £21.00 (£17.00 in the Family Stand)
Concessionary Seating: £13.00
Under-19s/Senior Citizen Standing: £6 – £8 (Members)
Away Supporters: £16.00 Standing; £17.00 Seating
Family Tickets: Available in the Family Stand when purchased in advance: £30.00 (2 adults + 2 Under-19s)
Programme Price: £3.00

DISABLED INFORMATION

Wheelchairs: 8 covered spaces in total for Home and Away fans on the North Terrace – Barnet Lane Entrance
Helpers: One helper admitted per wheelchair
Prices: £17.00 for each fan with a wheelchair
Disabled Toilets: One available in the Social Club
Are Bookings Necessary: 24 hours notice required
Contact: (020) 8441-6932 (Tony Peck)

Travelling Supporters' Information:
Routes: The ground is situated off the Great North Road (A1000) at the foot of Barnet Hill near to the junction with Station Road (A110). Barnet Lane is on the west of the A1000 next to the Cricket Ground.

BARNSLEY FC

Founded: 1887 (**Entered League**: 1898)
Former Names: Barnsley St. Peter's
Nickname: 'Reds'
Ground: Oakwell Stadium, Barnsley   S71 1ET
Ground Capacity: 23,176 (All seats)
Record Attendance: 40,255 (15th February 1936)
Pitch Size: 110 × 72 yards

Colours: Red shirts with White shorts and Red socks
Telephone Nº: (01226) 211211
Ticket Office: 0871 226-6777 (calls cost 10p/minute)
Fax Number: (01226) 211444
Web Site: www.barnsleyfc.co.uk
E-mail: thereds@barnsleyfc.co.uk

GENERAL INFORMATION

Car Parking: Queen's Ground Car Park (adjacent)
Coach Parking: Queen's Ground Car Park
Nearest Railway Station: Barnsley Interchange (6 minutes walk)
Nearest Bus Station: Barnsley Interchange
Club Shop: At the Stadium
Opening Times: Monday to Friday 9.00am to 5.00pm. Saturdays 9.00am to 2.00pm. Saturday Matchdays open 9.00am to 3.00pm then 4.45pm to 5.15pm. Evening matchdays open 9.00am to 7.45pm
Telephone Nº: (01226) 211400

GROUND INFORMATION

Away Supporters' Entrances & Sections:
North Stand Turnstiles 42-51

ADMISSION INFO (2012/2013 PRICES)

Adult Seating: £25.00 – £28.00
Under-12s Seating: £7.00
Concessionary Seating: £17.00 – £18.00
Note: Members are charged lower prices.
Programme Price: £3.00

DISABLED INFORMATION

Wheelchairs: A disabled stand provides accommodation to those in wheelchairs and blind supporters.
Helpers: Admitted depending on room available
Prices: £16.00 – £30.00 for the disabled but helpers are admitted free of charge
Disabled Toilets: Available in the Corner Stand, North Stand and C.K. Beckett Stand
Commentaries are available for the blind
Contact: 0871 226-6777 (Bookings are necessary)

Travelling Supporters' Information: From All Parts: Exit the M1 at Junction 37 and follow the 'Barnsley FC/Football Ground' signs which lead to a large surface car park adjacent to the stadium (2 miles).

BIRMINGHAM CITY FC

Founded: 1875 (**Entered League**: 1892)
Former Names: Small Heath Alliance FC (1875-88); Small Heath FC (1888-1905); Birmingham FC (1905-45)
Nickname: 'Blues'
Ground: St. Andrew's Stadium, Birmingham B9 4RL
Ground Capacity: 29,409 (All seats)
Record Attendance: 68,844 (11th February 1939)

Pitch Size: 120 × 72 yards (110 × 66 metres)
Colours: Royal Blue Shirts and Shorts
Telephone N°: 0844 557-1875
Ticket Office: 0844 557-1875 Option 2
Fax Number: 0844 557-1975
Web Site: www.bcfc.com
Web Site: reception@bcfc.com

GENERAL INFORMATION

Car Parking: Street Parking + Birmingham Wheels (secure parking but not related to the club)
Coach Parking: Coventry Road
Nearest Railway Station: Birmingham New Street or Birmingham Moor Street (20 minutes walk)
Nearest Bus Station: Digbeth National Express Coach Station
Club Shops: St. Andrew's Superstore at the ground
Opening Times: Monday to Saturday 9.30am to 5.30pm
Telephone N°: 0844 557-1875 Option 4

GROUND INFORMATION

Away Supporters' Entrances & Sections:
Gil Merrick Stand, Coventry Road

ADMISSION INFO (2011/2012 PRICES)

Adult Seating: £16.00 – £40.00
Senior Citizen/Child Seating: £5.00 – £30.00
Note: Prices vary depending on the category of the match and the location of the seat.
Programme Price: £3.00

DISABLED INFORMATION

Wheelchairs: Spaces available in the Spion Kop Stand, Family Stand, Gil Merrick Lower Stand and Tilton Road Stand
Helpers: One assistant admitted for each disabled fan
Prices: £10.00 – £22.00 for each disabled adult fan and £5.00 – £11.00 for each disabled child/senior citizen fan (prices depend on the category of the match).
Disabled Toilets: Available in the Spion Kop Stand, Family Stand, Gil Merrick Stand and Tilton Road Stand
Contact: 0844 557-1875 Option 2 (Bookings are necessary)

Travelling Supporters' Information: From All Parts: Exit M6 at Junction 6 and take the A38 (M) (Aston Expressway). Leave at 2nd exit then take first exit at roundabout along the Dartmouth Middleway. After 1¼ miles turn left on to Coventry Road.
Bus Services: Services 96 & 97 from Birmingham; Services 98 & 99 from Digbeth.

BLACKBURN ROVERS FC

Founded: 1875 (**Entered League**: 1888)
Nickname: 'Rovers' 'Blues & Whites'
Ground: Ewood Park, Blackburn,
Lancashire BB2 4JF
Pitch Size: 115 × 72 yards
Ground Capacity: 31,154 (All seats)
Record Attendance: 62,255 vs Bolton (2/3/1929)

Colours: Blue and White halved shirts, White shorts
Telephone Nº: 0871 702-1875
Ticket Office: 0871 222-1444
Fax Number: (01254) 671042
Web Site: www.rovers.co.uk

GENERAL INFORMATION

Car Parking: 800 spaces available at the ground
Coach Parking: At the ground
Nearest Railway Station: Blackburn Central (1½ miles)
Nearest Bus Station: Blackburn Central (1½ miles)
Club Shop: At the ground and in the Town Centre
Opening Times: Ewood Shop: Monday to Friday 9.00am –
5.30pm, Saturday 10.00am–4.00pm closed on Sundays.
Town Centre Shop: Monday to Friday 9.00am – 5.30pm,
Satruday open all day and Sunday 11.00am – 4.00pm
Telephone Nº: (01254) 296137 (Ewood shop)

GROUND INFORMATION

Away Supporters' Entrances & Sections: Darwen End

ADMISSION INFO (2011/2012 PRICES)

Adult Seating: £15.00 – £40.00
Child Seating: £5.00 – £20.00
Concessions Seating: £10.00 – £30.00
Student Seating: £10.00 – £17.00
Note: Prices vary depending on the category of the game
Programme Price: £3.00

DISABLED INFORMATION

Wheelchairs: 262 spaces in total for Home and Away fans
Helpers: One helper admitted per disabled fan. Please note
that applications for helpers tickets must be made in advance
Prices: Normal prices apply for the disabled and helpers
Disabled Toilets: 14 purpose-built ground level toilets
Commentaries available by arrangement for up to 6 people
Contact: 0871 702-1875 (Bookings are necessary)

Travelling Supporters' Information: Routes: Supporters travelling Northbound on the M6: Exit the M6 at Junction 29,
follow the M65 and exit at Junction 4 for Ewood Park. The ground is ¾ mile from Junction 4 – please look for parking areas to
avoid congestion around the ground; Supporters travelling Northbound on the M61: Exit the M61 at Junction 9, join the M65
and exit at Junction 4 (then as above); Supporters travelling Southbound on the M6: Exit the M6 at Junction 30, follow the
M61 and exit at Junction 9 onto the M65. Exit the M65 at Junction 4 for the ground; Supporters from the Yorkshire Area either
on the B6234, the A56 Haslingden by-pass or the A59 Skipton Road – please follow signs for Ewood Park (follow Preston M65
and exit at Junction 4).

BLACKPOOL FC

Founded: 1887 **(Entered League**: 1896)
Former Name: Merged with Blackpool St.Johns (1887)
Nickname: 'Seasiders' or 'Tangerines'
Ground: Bloomfield Road, Blackpool, FY1 6JJ
Ground Capacity: 16,000 (All seats)
Record Attendance: 38,098 (17th September 1955)
Pitch Size: 110 × 74 yards

Colours: Tangerine shirts with White shorts
Telephone Nº: 0870 443-1953
Ticket Office: 0870 443-1953
Fax Number: (01253) 405011
Web Site: www.blackpoolfc.co.uk

GENERAL INFORMATION
Car Parking: 3,000 spaces at the ground and street parking
Coach Parking: Available at the ground
Nearest Railway Station: Blackpool South (5 mins. walk)
Nearest Bus Station: Talbot Road (2 miles)
Club Shop: At the ground
Opening Times: Daily from 9.00am to 5.15pm
Telephone Nº: 0870 443-1953

GROUND INFORMATION
Away Supporters' Entrances & Sections:
East Stand (Uncovered)

ADMISSION INFO (2012/2013 PRICES)
Adult Seating: £24.00 – £25.00
Ages 16 to 18 Seating: £16.00 – £17.00
Under-16s Seating: £13.00 – £15.00
Under-12s Seating: £11.00 (Family Stand only)
Senior Citizen Seating: £19.00 – £20.00
Note: A transaction fee is charged for telephone bookings
Programme Price: £3.00

DISABLED INFORMATION
Wheelchairs: Over 50 spaces in total for home and away
fans in the new North and West Stands
Helpers: One helper admitted per disabled fan
Prices: £12.00 for the disabled
Disabled Toilets: Available
Contact: 0870 443-1953 (Bookings are necessary)

Travelling Supporters' Information: From All Parts: Exit M6 at Junction 32 onto the M55. Follow signs for the main car parks along the new 'spine' road to the car parks at the side of the ground.

BOLTON WANDERERS FC

Founded: 1874 (**Entered League**: 1888)
Former Names: Christchurch FC (1874-1877)
Nickname: 'Trotters'
Ground: Reebok Stadium, Burnden Way, Lostock, Bolton, Lancashire   BL6 6JW
Ground Capacity: 27,879 (All seats)
Pitch Size: 110 × 70 yards

Record Attendance: 27,409
Colours: White shirts with Navy Blue shorts
Telephone Nº: 0844 871-2932
Ticket Office: 0844 871-2932
Fax Number: 0871 871-8183
Web Site: www.bwfc.co.uk
E-mail: reception@bwfc.co.uk

GENERAL INFORMATION
Car Parking: 2,800 spaces available at the ground
Coach Parking: Available at the ground
Nearest Railway Station: Horwich Parkway (600 yards)
Nearest Bus Station: Moor Lane, Bolton
Club Shop: At the ground
Opening Times: Daily from 9.30am to 5.30pm
Telephone Nº: (01204) 673650

GROUND INFORMATION
Away Supporters' Entrances & Sections:
South Stand entrances and accommodation

ADMISSION INFO (2011/2012 PRICES)
Adult Seating: £20.00 – £38.00
Child Seating: £9.00 – £20.00
Senior Citizen Seating: £15.00 – £27.00
Note: Prices vary depending on the category of the game and special family tickets are also available
Programme Price: £3.00

DISABLED INFORMATION
Wheelchairs: 32 spaces available for visiting fans, 72 spaces for home fans
Helpers: One helper admitted per disabled fan
Prices: Free for wheelchair users. Helpers normal prices
Disabled Toilets: Yes
Contact: 0844 871-2932   (Bookings are necessary)

Travelling Supporters' Information:
From All Parts: Exit the M61 at Junction 6 and the ground is clearly visible ¼ mile away.

BRADFORD CITY FC

Founded: 1903 (**Entered League**: 1903)
Nickname: 'Bantams'
Ground: Coral Windows Stadium, Valley Parade, Bradford   BD8 7DY
Ground Capacity: 25,134 (All seats)
Record Attendance: 39,146 (11th March 1911)
Pitch Size: 113 × 70 yards

Colours: Claret and Amber shirts with Claret shorts
Telephone Nº: 0871 978-1911
Ticket Office: 0871-978-8000
Fax Number: (01274) 773356
Web Site: www.bradfordcityfc.co.uk
E-mail: bradfordcityfc@compuserve.com

GENERAL INFORMATION
Car Parking: Street Parking and Car Parks (£3.00 charge)
Coach Parking: By Police direction
Nearest Railway Station: Bradford Foster Square
Nearest Bus Station: Bradford Interchange (1 mile)
Club Shop: At the ground
Opening Times: Monday to Friday 9.30am to 5.00pm, Saturday 9.00am to 3.00pm
Telephone Nº: (01274) 309945

GROUND INFORMATION
Away Supporters' Entrances & Sections:
Midland Road Stand entrances and accommodation

ADMISSION INFO (2012/2013 PRICES)
Adult Seating: £20.00
Under-16s Seating: £12.00
Senior Citizen Seating: £14.00
Programme Price: £3.00

DISABLED INFORMATION
Wheelchairs: 100 spaces available in total for Home and Away fans in the disabled area, 'A' Block of Sunwin Stand and also in the Carlsberg Stand & East Stand
Helpers: One helper admitted per disabled fan
Prices: Normal prices for disabled fans. Helpers admitted free
Disabled Toilets: Available behind the disabled area
Contact: 0871 978-8000 (Bookings are necessary)

Travelling Supporters' Information: Routes: Exit the M62 at Junction 26 and take the M606 towards Bradford. At the end of the motorway get in the middle lane and follow signs for Bradford (West) into Rooley Lane (signs for the Airport). A McDonalds is now on your left. Turn left into Wakefield Road at the roundabout and stay in the middle lane. Continue straight on over two roundabouts (signs to Shipley and Skipton) onto Shipley Airedale Road which then becomes Canal Road. Just after Tesco on the left, turn left into Station Road and left again into Queens Road. Go up the hill to the third set of traffic lights and turn left into Manningham Lane. After the Gulf petrol station on the left, turn first left into Valley Parade for the Stadium.

BRENTFORD FC

Founded: 1889 (**Entered League**: 1920)
Nickname: 'The Bees'
Ground: Griffin Park, Braemar Road, Brentford, Middlesex TW8 0NT
Ground Capacity: 12,800
Seating Capacity: 10,200
Record Attendance: 38,678 (26th February 1949)

Pitch Size: 110 × 74 yards
Colours: Red & White striped shirts with Black shorts
Telephone Nº: 0845 3456-442
Ticket Office: 0845 3456-442
Fax Number: (020) 8568-9940
Web Site: www.brentfordfc.co.uk
E-mail: enquiries@brentfordfc.co.uk

GENERAL INFORMATION
Car Parking: Street Parking
Coach Parking: By Police direction
Nearest Railway Station: Brentford (½ mile)
Nearest Tube Station: South Ealing (Piccadilly) (1 mile)
Club Shop: Adjacent to the ground in Braemar Road
Opening Times: Weekdays 10.00am–4.00pm and Matchdays 12.00pm – 6.00pm
Telephone Nº: 0845 3456-442

GROUND INFORMATION
Away Supporters' Entrances & Sections:
Brook Road Upper and Lower for both seating and terracing

ADMISSION INFO (2012/2013 PRICES)
Adult Standing: £19.00 – £21.00
Adult Seating: £20.00 – £23.00
Juniors Standing/Seating: £5.00
Senior Citizen Standing: £13.00 – £15.00
Senior Citizen Seating: £14.00 – £17.00
Student Standing: £11.00 – £13.00
Student Seating: £12.00 – £15.00
Programme Price: £3.00

DISABLED INFORMATION
Wheelchairs: 10 spaces for Home fans, 2 spaces for Away fans in the disabled section, Braemar Road
Helpers: One helper admitted per disabled fan
Prices: Normal prices for the disabled. Free for helpers
Disabled Toilets: Available in the disabled section
Commentaries are available for the blind
Contact: 0845 3456-442 (Bookings are necessary)

Travelling Supporters' Information: Routes: From the North: Take the A406 North Circular (from the M1/A1) to the Chiswick Roundabout and then along the Great West Road and turn left at the third set of traffic lights into Ealing Road for the ground; From the East: Take the A406 to the Chiswick Roundabout, then as North; From the West: Exit M4 at Junction 2 – down to the Chiswick Roundabout, then as North; From the South: Use the A3, M3, A240 or A316 to Kew Road, continue along over Kew Bridge, turn left at the traffic lights, then right at the next traffic lights into Ealing Road.

BRIGHTON & HOVE ALBION FC

Founded: 1901 (**Entered League**: 1920)
Nickname: 'Seagulls'
Ground: American Express Community Stadium, Village Way, Brighton BN1 9BL
Ground Capacity: 22,374 (All seats)
Pitch Size: 115 × 75 yards
Record Attendance: 8,691 (at Withdean Stadium)

Colours: Blue & White striped shirts with White shorts
Telephone Nº: (01273) 878288
Ticket Office: 0845 496-1901
Fax Number: (01273) 878238
Web Site: www.seagulls.co.uk
E-mail: feedback@bhafc.co.uk

GENERAL INFORMATION

Car Parking: Limited parking at the stadium and 700 spaces available at the University campus (adjacent)
Coach Parking: At the stadium
Nearest Railway Station: Falmer (adjacent)
Nearest Bus Station: Brighton
Club Shop: At the stadium and also at 128 Queen's Road, Brighton, BN1 3WB
Opening Times: Monday to Saturday 9.30am – 5.30pm (shop closes at 5.00pm on Home matchdays)
Telephone Nº: 0845 496-9442

GROUND INFORMATION

Away Supporters' Entrances & Sections:
South Stand

ADMISSION INFO (2012/2013 PRICES)

Adult Seating: £28.00 – £39.00
Under-10s Seating: £7.00 – £10.00 (£4.00 in Family Stand)
Under-16s Seating: £7.00 in Family Stand when accompanied by a paying Adult
Under-18s Seating: £14.00 – £19.00
Senior Citizen Seating: £20.00 – £26.00
Programme Price: £3.00

DISABLED INFORMATION

Wheelchairs: Approximately 250 spaces available in total
Helpers: One helper admitted per disabled person
Prices: Normal prices for the disabled. Free for helpers
Disabled Toilets: Yes – in all the stands
Contact: 0845 496-1901 (Bookings are necessary)

Travelling Supporters' Information: Routes: From the North: Take the M23 then the A23 to Brighton. At the roundabout on the outskirts of Brighton, take the exit onto the A27 towards Lewes. Pass the A270 turn-off and continue towards the village of Falmer. The stadium is situated by the side of the A27 in the village of Falmer across the road from the University of Sussex campus; From the East and West: Take the A27 to Falmer which is located to the north-east of Brighton. Then as above.

BRISTOL CITY FC

Founded: 1894 (**Entered League**: 1901)
Former Name: Bristol South End FC (1894-1897)
Nickname: 'The Robins'
Ground: Ashton Gate Stadium, Bristol   BS3 2EJ
Ground Capacity: 21,497 (All seats)
Pitch Size: 115 × 75 yards
Record Attendance: 43,335 (16th February 1935)

Colours: Red shirts with White shorts
Telephone N°: 0871 222-6666
Ticket Hotline: 0871 222-6666 (Option 1)
Fax Number: (0117) 963-0700
Web Site: www.bcfc.co.uk
E-mail: enquiries@bcfc.co.uk

GENERAL INFORMATION

Car Parking: Street parking
Coach Parking: By prior arrangement with the club
Nearest Railway Station: Bristol Temple Meads (1½ miles)
Nearest Bus Station: Bristol City Centre
Club Shop: BCFC Megastore at the ground
Opening Times: Monday 10.00am to 5.00pm, Tuesday to Friday 9.00am to 5.00pm and Saturdays 9.00am to 3.00pm (open until kick-off on Matchdays)
Telephone N°: 0871 222-6666 (Option 1)

GROUND INFORMATION

Away Supporters' Entrances & Sections:
Wedlock Stand

ADMISSION INFO (2012/2013 PRICES)

Adult Seating: £25.00 – £30.00
Under-16s Seating: £12.00 – £15.00
Concessionary Seating: £20.00 – £25.00
Note: A membership scheme is available which offers discounted prices for advance bookings
Programme Price: £3.00

DISABLED INFORMATION

Wheelchairs: Limited number accommodated at pitchside – please apply early
Helpers: One helper admitted per disabled fan
Prices: Normal prices for the disabled. Free for helpers
Disabled Toilets: Available in various areas of the ground
Commentaries are available for the blind (contact the club for further information)
Contact: 0871 222-6666 Option 1 (Bookings are necessary)

Travelling Supporters' Information: Routes: From the North & West: Exit the M5 at Junction 16, take the A38 to Bristol City Centre and follow the A38 Taunton signs. Cross the swing bridge after 1¼ miles and bear left into Winterstoke Road for the ground; From the East: Take the M4 then M32 and follow signs for the City Centre. Then as for North and West; From the South: Exit the M5 at Junction 19 and follow Taunton signs over the swing bridge (then as above).
Away Fans Car Parking: Bedminster Cricket Club, Clanidge Road, Bristol – SatNav: BS3 2JX (½ mile from Ashton Gate)
Bus Services: Services 27A and 28A from Bristol Temple Meads Station. A bus leaves Temple Meads 1 hour prior to kick-off.

BRISTOL ROVERS FC

Founded: 1883 (**Entered League**: 1920)
Former Names: Black Arabs FC (1883-84);
Eastville Rovers FC (1884-96);
Bristol Eastville Rovers FC (1896-97)
Nickname: 'Pirates' 'Rovers' 'Gas'
Ground: Memorial Stadium, Filton Avenue, Horfield,
Bristol   BS7 0BF
Pitch Size: 110 × 71 yards

Ground Capacity: 11,917
Seating Capacity: 3,307
Record Attendance: 12,011 (9th March 2008)
Colours: Blue & White quartered shirts, White shorts
Telephone Nº: (0117) 909-6648
Fax Number: (0117) 908-5530
Web Site: www.bristolrovers.co.uk

GENERAL INFORMATION

Car Parking: Very limited number of spaces at the ground
and street parking
Coach Parking: At the ground
Nearest Railway Station: Temple Meads (2 miles)
Nearest Bus Station: Bristol City Centre
Club Shop: 199 Two Mile Hill Road, Kingswood and also at
Pirate Leisure, Memorial Stadium, Filton Avenue
Opening Times: Supporters' Club: Weekdays 9.00am to
5.00pm and Saturdays 9.00am to 1.00pm; Pirate Leisure:
Weekdays 9.00am to 5.00pm, Saturdays 9.00am to 1.00pm
(Home matchdays 9.00am – 3.00pm then 4.45pm – 5.15pm)
Telephone Nº: (0117) 961-1772 + (0117) 909-6648

GROUND INFORMATION

Away Supporters' Entrances & Sections:
Entrance to Uplands Terrace & South Stand via Filton Avenue

ADMISSION INFO (2012/2013 PRICES)

Adult Standing: £18.00 – £20.00
Adult Seating: £20.50 – £26.00
Concessionary Standing: £7.00 – £11.00
Concessionary Seating: £11.50 – £20.50
Note: A discount of £2.00 per ticket is available if purchased
prior to the matchday.
Programme Price: £3.00

DISABLED INFORMATION

Wheelchairs: Unspecified number accommodated in front
of the Uplands Stand and DAS Stand
Helpers: One helper admitted per disabled person
Prices: £11.00 for wheelchair and ambulant disabled.
Helpers are admitted free of charge
Disabled Toilets: In the Uplands Stand and DAS Stand
Contact: (0117) 909-6648 Option 1 (Bookings are necessary)

Travelling Supporters' Information: Routes: From All Parts: Exit the M32 at Junction 2 then take the exit at the roundabout
(signposted Horfield) into Muller Road. Continue for approximately 1½ miles passing straight across 3 sets of traffic lights. At the
6th set of traffic lights turn left into Filton Avenue and the ground is immediately on the left.

BURNLEY FC

Founded: 1882 (**Entered League**: 1888)
Former Name: Burnley Rovers FC
Nickname: 'Clarets'
Ground: Turf Moor, Harry Potts Way, Burnley,
Lancashire   BB10 4BX
Ground Capacity: 21,942 (All seats)
Record Attendance: 54,775 (23rd February 1924)

Pitch Size: 113 × 71 yards
Colours: Claret and Blue shirts with White shorts
Telephone Nº: 0871 221-1882
Ticket Office: 0871 221-1914
Fax Number: (01282) 700014
Web Site: www.burnleyfc.com
E-mail: info@burnleyfc.com

GENERAL INFORMATION

Car Parking: Matchday parking restrictions in surrounding streets so it is recommended that the various Town Centre car parks are used by visiting fans.
Coach Parking: By Police direction
Nearest Railway Station: Burnley Central (1½ miles)
Nearest Bus Station: Burnley (5 minutes walk)
Club Shop: At the ground
Opening Times: Monday to Friday 9.00am – 6.00pm;
Saturdays 9.00am – 5.00pm
Telephone Nº: 0871 221-1882

GROUND INFORMATION

Away Supporters' Entrances & Sections:
David Fishwick Stand

ADMISSION INFO (2012/2013 PRICES)

Adult Seating: £25.00 – £31.00
Under-16s Seating: £11.00 – £14.00
Concessionary Seating: £14.00 – £19.00
Note: Prices vary depending on the category of the game
Programme Price: £3.00

DISABLED INFORMATION

Wheelchairs: Three designated wheelchair areas
Helpers: One helper admitted for each wheelchair user
Prices: Normal prices apply for disabled fans plus one helper admitted free of charge
Disabled Toilets: Available
Commentaries are available via headsets (limited number)
Non-wheelchair disabled, please phone for further details
Contact: 0871 221-1914   (Bookings are necessary)

Travelling Supporters' Information: Routes: From the North: Follow the A682 to the Town Centre and take first exit at roundabout (Gala Club) into Yorkshire Street. Follow through traffic signals into Harry Potts Way; From the East: Follow the A646 to the A671 then along Todmorden Road towards the Town Centre. At the traffic signals (crossroads) turn right into Harry Potts Way; From the West & South: Exit the M6 at Junction 29 onto the M65. Exit the M65 at Junction 10 and follow signs for Burnley Football Club. At the roundabout in the town centre take the third exit into Yorkshire Street. Then as from the North.

BURTON ALBION FC

Founded: 1950   (**Entered League**: 2009)
Former Names: None
Nickname: 'The Brewers'
Ground: The Pirelli Stadium, Princess Way, Burton-on-Trent   DE13 0AR
Record Attendance: 6,192 (17th April 2009)
Pitch Size: 110 × 72 yards

Colours: Shirts are Yellow with Black trim, shorts are Black with Yellow Trim
Telephone N°: (01283) 565938
Fax Number: (01283) 523199
Ground Capacity: 6,972   **Seating Capacity**: 2,000
Web site: www.burtonalbionfc.co.uk
E-mail: bafc@burtonalbionfc.co.uk

GENERAL INFORMATION

Supporters Club: c/o Club
Telephone N°: (01283) 565938
Car Parking: Available at the ground
Coach Parking: Rykneld Trading Estate, Derby Road
Nearest Railway Station: Burton-on-Trent (1½ miles)
Nearest Bus Station: Burton-on-Trent (1½ miles)
Club Shop: At the ground
Opening Times: Weekdays 9.00am to 5.30pm and Matchdays from 1½ hours before kick-off
Telephone N°: (01283) 565938

GROUND INFORMATION

Away Supporters' Entrances & Sections:
East Stand, Derby Road

ADMISSION INFO (2012/2013 PRICES)

Adult Standing: £14.00
Adult Seating: £16.00
Child Standing: £4.00
Child Seating: £6.00
Senior Citizen Standing: £12.00
Senior Citizen Seating: £14.00
Programme Price: £3.00

DISABLED INFORMATION

Wheelchairs: Over 78 spaces available for home and away fans in the designated disabled areas
Helpers: Admitted
Prices: Normal prices for the disabled. Free for helpers
Disabled Toilets: Available in all stands
Contact: (01283) 565938   (Bookings are necessary)

Travelling Supporters' Information:
Routes: From the M1, North and South: Exit at Junction 23A and join the A50 towards Derby (also signposted for Alton Towers). Join the A38 southbound at the Toyota factory (towards Burton & Lichfield) then exit for Burton North onto the A5121. Continue past the Pirelli factory on the right and the BP Garage and Cash & Carry on the left then turn into Princess Way at the roundabout; From the M5/6 South: Join the M42 northbound and exit onto the A446 signposted Lichfield. Follow signs for the A38 to Burton then exit onto A5121 as above; From the M6 North: Exit at Junction 15 and follow the A50 towards Stoke and Uttoxeter. Exit the A50 for the A38 southbound signposted Burton and Lichfield at the Toyota factory, then as above.

BURY FC

Founded: 1885 (**Entered League**: 1894)
Nickname: 'Shakers'
Ground: Gigg Lane, Bury, Lancashire BL9 9HR
Ground Capacity: 11,313 (All seats)
Pitch Size: 112 × 70 yards
Record Attendance: 35,000 (9th January 1960)

Colours: White shirts with Royal Blue shorts & socks
Telephone Nº: 0844 579-0009
Ticket Office: 0844 579-0009
General Fax Number: (0161) 764-5521
Commercial Dept. Fax Number: (0161) 763-3103
Web Site: www.buryfc.co.uk
E-mail: admin@buryfc.co.uk

GENERAL INFORMATION
Car Parking: Designated car parks only
Coach Parking: By Police direction
Nearest Railway Station: Bury Interchange (1 mile)
Nearest Bus Station: Bury Interchange
Club Shop: At the ground
Opening Times: Monday to Friday and Saturday matchdays 10.00am to 5.00pm. Closed on Wednesdays.
Telephone Nº: (0161) 762-0528

GROUND INFORMATION
Away Supporters' Entrances & Sections:
Gigg Lane entrance for the West Stand

ADMISSION INFO (2012/2013 PRICES)
Adult Seating: £17.00 – £21.00
Under-16s/Over-65s Seating: £10.00 – £12.00
Young Persons Seating (Ages 16-21): £13.00 – £15.00
Note: Prices vary depending on the category of the game and some family concessions are also available
Programme Price: £3.00

DISABLED INFORMATION
Wheelchairs: Spaces for 46 wheelchairs in disabled sections (home area) and a further 8 spaces in the Away Supporters' Section
Helpers: One helper admitted per wheelchair
Prices: £10.00 – £12.00 for the disabled. Free for helpers
Disabled Toilets: Available in disabled section
A Radio Commentary is available in the Press Box for the Registered Blind
Contact: 0844 579-0009   (Bookings are not necessary)

Travelling Supporters' Information: Routes: From the North: Exit the M66 at Junction 2, take Bury Road (A58) for ½ mile, then turn left into Heywood Street and follow this into Parkhills Road until its end, turn left into Manchester Road (A56) and then left again into Gigg Lane. From the South, East and West: Exit the M60 at Junction 17, take Bury Road (A56) for 3 miles and then turn right into Gigg Lane.

CARDIFF CITY FC

Founded: 1899 (**Entered League**: 1920)
Former Names: Riverside FC (1899-1902) and Riverside Albion FC (1902-1908)
Nickname: 'Bluebirds'
Ground: Cardiff City Stadium, Cardiff CF11 8SX
Record Attendance: 26,058 (23rd April 2011)
Ground Capacity: 26,828 (All seats)

Pitch Size: 110 × 75 yards
Colours: Royal Blue shirts with White shorts
Telephone Nº: 0845 345-1400
Away Support Ticket Office: 0845 345-1405
Fax Number: (029) 2034-1148
Web Site: www.cardiffcityfc.co.uk
E-mail: club@cardiffcityfc.co.uk

GENERAL INFORMATION

Car Parking: Stadium car park and Street Parking
Coach Parking: Stadium car park (adjacent)
Nearest Railway Station: Cardiff Central (1 mile) and also Ninian Park Station (500 yards)
Nearest Bus Station: Cardiff Central
Club Shop: At the ground
Opening Times: Weekdays from 9.00am to 2.00pm and Matchdays 10.00am to 2.00pm
Telephone Nº: 0845 345-1485
Postal Sales: Yes (Internet Sales also accepted)

GROUND INFORMATION

Away Supporters' Entrances & Sections:
Grange End, Gate 07 – sections 119 to 122

ADMISSION INFO (2012/2013 PRICES)

For the 2012/2013 season, Cardiff City are operating a demand-based pricing system so prices will vary depending on the demand for tickets and the date at which they are purchased. Please contact the club for further pricing details about individual games.
Programme Price: £3.00

DISABLED INFORMATION

Wheelchairs: Numerous spaces available for disabled supporters in various areas around the ground
Helpers: One helper admitted per disabled fan
Prices: Normal prices for the disabled. Helpers admitted free of charge
Disabled Toilets: Available
Contact: 0845 345-1400 (Away fans tickets are normally sold in advance but may be available on the day)

Travelling Supporters' Information:
Routes: From All Parts: Exit M4 at Junction 33 and follow Penarth (A4232) signs. After 6 miles, take the B4267 to Cardiff City Stadium.

CARLISLE UNITED FC

Founded: 1903 (**Entered League**: 1928)
Former Names: Formed with the amalgamation of Shaddongate United FC and Carlisle Red Rose FC
Nickname: 'Cumbrians' 'Blues'
Ground: Brunton Park Stadium, Warwick Road, Carlisle   CA1 1LL
Ground Capacity: 17,902
Seating Capacity: 7,594

Record Attendance: 27,500 (5th January 1957)
Pitch Size: 112 × 74 yards
Colours: Royal Blue and White shirts and shorts
Telephone Nº: (01228) 526237
Ticket Office: 0844 371-1921
Fax Number: (01228) 554141
Web Site: www.carlisleunited.co.uk
E-mail: enquiries@carlisleunited.co.uk

GENERAL INFORMATION

Car Parking: Rear of Ground via St. Aidans Road
Coach Parking: St. Aidans Road Car Park
Nearest Railway Station: Carlisle Citadel (1 mile)
Nearest Bus Station: Lowther Street, Carlisle
Club Shop: At the ground and in the City Centre
Opening Times: Monday to Saturday 10.00am – 5.30pm
Telephone Nº: (01228) 554138

GROUND INFORMATION

Away Supporters' Entrances & Sections:
Turnstiles 14-16 for the Petteril End or CBS Stand Section 2

ADMISSION INFO (2012/2013 PRICES)

Adult Standing: £16.00 – £19.00 **Seating**: £19 – £22
Ages 18-22 Standing: £10.00–£13.00 **Seating**: £13–£16
Ages 11-17 Standing: £7.00–£10.00 **Seating**: £10–£13
Under-11s Standing: £4.00   **Under-11s Seating**: £7.00
Under-7s: Admitted free of charge
Senior Citizen Standing: £14.00
Senior Citizen Seating: £16.00
Note: Tickets are cheaper if purchased before the matchday
Programme Price: £3.00

DISABLED INFORMATION

Wheelchairs: 17 spaces for wheelchairs in the disabled section, in front of the New East Stand
Helpers: One helper admitted per disabled fan
Prices: Wheelchair disabled are admitted for £4.00. Helpers are admitted free of charge.
Disabled Toilets: Available
Contact: (01228) 526237   (Bookings are recommended)

Travelling Supporters' Information:
Routes: From the North, South and East: Exit the M6 at Junction 43 and follow signs for Carlisle (A69) into Warwick Road for the ground; From the West: Take the A69 straight into Warwick Road.

CHARLTON ATHLETIC FC

Founded: 1905 (**Entered League**: 1921)
Nickname: 'Addicks'
Ground: The Valley, Floyd Road, Charlton, London, SE7 8BL
Ground Capacity: 27,111 (All seats)
Record Attendance: 75,031 (12th February 1938)
Pitch Size: 111 × 73 yards

Colours: Red shirts with White shorts
Telephone Nº: (020) 8333-4000
Ticket Office: 0871 226-1905
Fax Number: (020) 8333-4001
Web Site: www.cafc.co.uk
E-mail: customerservices@cafc.co.uk

GENERAL INFORMATION

Car Parking: Street Parking
Coach Parking: By Police direction
Nearest Railway Station: Charlton (2 minutes walk)
Nearest Bus Station: At Charlton Railway Station as above
Club Shop: At the ground
Opening Times: Weekdays 10.00am – 5.00pm
Non-Match Saturdays 10.00am – 4.00pm
Telephone Nº: (020) 8333-4035

GROUND INFORMATION

Away Supporters' Entrances & Sections:
Valley Grove/Jimmy Seed Stand

ADMISSION INFO (2012/2013 PRICES)

Adult Seating: £18.00 – £25.00
Under-18s Seating: £10.00
Under-11s Seating: £5.00
Concessionary Seating: £13.00 – £18.00
Programme Price: £3.00

DISABLED INFORMATION

Wheelchairs: 96 spaces available for Home fans in the West and East Stands. 7 spaces available for Away fans in the South (Jimmy Seed) Stand
Helpers: One helper admitted per disabled fan
Prices: Helpers are admitted free of charge. Wheelchair disabled pay concessionary prices
Disabled Toilets: Available in West and East Stands
Commentaries are available – please ring for details
Contact: 0871 226-1905 (Bookings are necessary)

Travelling Supporters' Information:
Routes: From All Parts: Exit the M25 at Junction 2 (A2 London-bound) and follow until the road becomes the A102(M). Take the exit marked Woolwich Ferry and turn right along the A206 Woolwich Road. After approximately 1 mile do a U-turn at the roundabout back along Woolwich Road. At the traffic lights turn left into Charlton Church Lane and Floyd Road is the 2nd left.

CHELSEA FC

Founded: 1905 (**Entered League**: 1905)
Nickname: 'Blues'
Ground: Stamford Bridge, Fulham Road, London, SW6 1HS
Ground Capacity: 41,837 (All seats)
Record Attendance: 82,905 (12th October 1935)
Pitch Size: 113 × 74 yards

Colours: Blue shirts and shorts
Telephone No: 0871 984-1955 (UK callers); +44 20-7386-9373 (International callers)
Fax Number: (020) 7381-4831
Web Site: www.chelseafc.com

GENERAL INFORMATION

Car Parking: Pre-booked underground car park at ground
Coach Parking: By Police direction
Nearest Tube Station: Fulham Broadway (District)
Club Shop: Chelsea Megastore – at the ground
Opening Times: Monday to Saturday 9.00am – 6.00pm; Sundays 11.00am–5.00pm; Bank Holidays 11.00am – 5.00pm Stadium tours are also available
Megastore Telephone No: (020) 7565-1490

GROUND INFORMATION

Away Supporters' Entrances & Sections:
Shed End

ADMISSION INFO (2012/2013 PRICES)

Adult Seating: £36.00 – £87.00
Child Seating: £15.50 – £27.50
Senior Citizen Seating: £15.50 – £27.50
Note: Concessionary priced tickets are available in the Family Stand and East Upper Stand
Programme Price: £3.00

DISABLED INFORMATION

Disabled Seating: 290 spaces in total (including personal assistants) for Home and Away fans in the disabled area
Personal Assistants: One admitted per disabled fan
Prices: Free of charge for the disabled (for rota members)
Disabled Toilets: Available in the East Stand Concourse, West Stand and also in the Matthew Harding Stand
Free commentaries for blind supporters are available
Contact: (020) 7915-1950   (Bookings are necessary)

Travelling Supporters' Information:
Routes: From the North & East: Follow Central London signs from the A1/M1 to Hyde Park Corner, then signs for Guildford (A3) to Knightsbridge (A4). After 1 mile turn left into Fulham Road; From the South: Take the A13 or A24 then the A219 to cross Putney Bridge and follow signs for 'West End' (A304) to join the A308 into Fulham Road; From the West: Take the M4 then A4 to Central London, then follow signs to Westminster (A3220). After ¾ mile, turn right at crossroads into Fulham Road.

CHELTENHAM TOWN FC

Founded: 1887 (**Entered League**: 1999)
Nickname: 'Robins'
Ground: Abbey Business Stadium, Whaddon Road, Cheltenham, Gloucestershire GL52 5NA
Ground Capacity: 7,136
Seating Capacity: 4,054
Record Attendance: 8,326 (1956)

Pitch Size: 110 × 72 yards
Colours: Ruby shirts and shorts
Telephone Nº: (01242) 573558
Fax Number: (01242) 224675
Web Site: www.ctfc.com
E-mail: info@ctfc.com

GENERAL INFORMATION

Car Parking: No parking is available at the ground.
A Park & Ride scheme runs from Cheltenham Race Course
Coach Parking: Please phone for details
Nearest Railway Station: Cheltenham Spa (2½ miles)
Nearest Bus Station: Cheltenham Royal Well
Club Shop: At the ground
Opening Times: Weekdays & Matchdays 10.00am–2.45pm.
Telephone Nº: (01242) 573558

GROUND INFORMATION

Away Supporters' Entrances & Sections:
Hazlewoods Stand (entrance from Whaddon Road) or the In2Print Stand

ADMISSION INFO (2012/2013 PRICES)

Adult Standing: £15.00 or £17.00
Adult Seating: £20.00 or £22.00
Child Standing: £5.00 or £7.00 (Under-16s)
Child Seating: £7.00 or £9.00 (Under-16s)
Concessionary Standing: £11.00 or £13.00
Concessionary Seating: £13.00 or £16.00
Programme Price: £3.00

DISABLED INFORMATION

Wheelchairs: Accommodated in front of the Main Stand (use main entrance) and in the In 2 Print Stand
Helpers: Admitted free of charge
Prices: Concessionary prices are charged
Disabled Toilets: Available in the In 2 Print Stand, adjacent to the Stagecoach West Stand and in the Social Club
Contact: (01242) 573558   (Bookings are necessary)

Travelling Supporters' Information:
Routes: The ground is situated to the North-East of Cheltenham, 1 mile from the Town Centre off the B4632 (Prestbury Road) – Whaddon Road is to the East of the B4632 just North of Pittville Circus. Road signs in the vicinity indicate 'Whaddon Road/ Cheltenham Town FC'.

CHESTERFIELD FC

Founded: 1866 (**Entered League**: 1899)
Former Names: Chesterfield Municipal FC, Chesterfield Town FC
Nickname: 'Spireites' 'Blues'
Ground: b2net stadium , 1866 Sheffield Road, Whittington Moor, Chesterfield   S41 8NZ
Ground Capacity: 10,300 (All seats)

Record Attendance: 30,968 (Saltergate – 7/4/1939)
Pitch Size: 115 × 75 yards
Colours: Blue shirts with White shorts
Telephone Nº: (01246) 209765
Ticket Office: (01246) 209765
Fax Number: (01246) 556799
Web Site: www.chesterfield-fc.co.uk

GENERAL INFORMATION

Car Parking: Various Car Parks available nearby
Coach Parking: At the ground
Nearest Railway Station: Chesterfield (1¼ miles)
Nearest Bus Station: Chesterfield
Club Shop: At the ground
Opening Times: Monday to Friday 9.00am to 5.00pm. Saturday 10.00am to 3.00pm on matchdays only
Telephone Nº: (01246) 209765

GROUND INFORMATION

Away Supporters' Entrances & Sections:
North (Printability Stand) Turnstiles

ADMISSION INFO (2012/2013 PRICES)

Adult Seating: £18.00 – £22.00
Juvenile (Under-15s) Seating: £5.00 – £10.00
Concessionary Seating: £12.00 – £17.00
Under-7s Seating: £2.00 in the Family Stand
Programme Price: £3.00

DISABLED INFORMATION

Wheelchairs: Up to 100 spaces available around the ground
Note: Lifts are available in the East and West stands
Helpers: One helper admitted per disabled fan as required
Prices: Concessionary prices for the disabled. One helper admitted free of charge with each disabled fan.
Disabled Toilets: Available in all stands
Contact: (01246) 209765   (Bookings are advised)

Travelling Supporters' Information:
Routes: From the South: Exit the M1 at Junction 29 and follow the A617 for Chesterfield. At the roundabout, take the 4th exit and head north on the A61 Sheffield Road and the stadium is located in the Whittington Moor district next to the junction with the A619; From the East: Take the A619 to Chesterfield and the ground is situated next to the Tesco supermarket at the junction with the A61; From the North: Exit the M1 at Junction 30 and take the A619 to Chesterfield. Then as above.

COLCHESTER UNITED FC

Founded: 1937 (**Entered League**: 1950)
Former Names: The Eagles FC & Colchester Town FC
Nickname: 'U's'
Ground: Weston Homes Community Stadium, United Way, Colchester CO4 5UP
Ground Capacity: 10,105 (All seats)
Record Attendance: 19,072 (27/11/48 – Layer Road)
Pitch Size: 112 × 72 yards

Colours: Royal blue & white striped shirts with Royal blue shorts and white socks
Telephone Nº: (01206) 755100
Ticket Office: 0845 437-9089
Fax Number: (01206) 755114
Web Site: www.cu-fc.com
E-mail: caroline@colchesterunited.net

GENERAL INFORMATION

Car Parking: 700 spaces at the ground – pre-bookings only. The club recommends fans should use the Matchday shuttle bus service (cost £1.50) where possible. This runs from Bruff Close, near Colchester North Railway Station where there is a large car park for all fans.
Coach Parking: Drivers should liaise with with stewards upon arrival at the ground
Nearest Railway Station: Colchester North (1½ miles)
Nearest Bus Station: Colchester Town Centre (1½ miles)
Club Shop: At the ground
Opening Times: Matchdays only 10.00am to 3.00pm then 5.00pm to 6.00pm.
Telephone Nº: 0845 437-9089

GROUND INFORMATION

Away Supporters' Entrances & Sections:
North Stand or East Stand (North End)

ADMISSION INFO (2012/2013 PRICES)

Adult Seating: £19.00 – £27.00
Concessionary Seating: £13.00 – £21.00
Under-18s Seating: £10.00 – £14.00
Under-14s Seating: £4.00 – £7.00
Under-8s Seating: £2.00 – £3.00
Note: Prices vary depending on the category of the game and discounted prices are available for advance purchases
Programme Price: £3.00

DISABLED INFORMATION

Wheelchairs: 40 spaces in total situated in all stands with lift access available where required.
Helpers: One helper admitted per wheelchair
Prices: £13.00 – £21.00 for each adult disabled fan. Helpers are admitted free of charge.
Disabled Toilets: Available in each stand
Contact: 0845 437-9089

Travelling Supporters' Information:
Routes: The stadium is located at junction 28 of the A12 on the northern outskirts of Colchester. As parking near the stadium is very limited, the club recommends both home and away fans should use the Matchday shuttle bus service which runs from Bruff Close, near to Colchester North Station where there is a large car park. Alternatively, pre-book a space in the club car park.

COVENTRY CITY FC

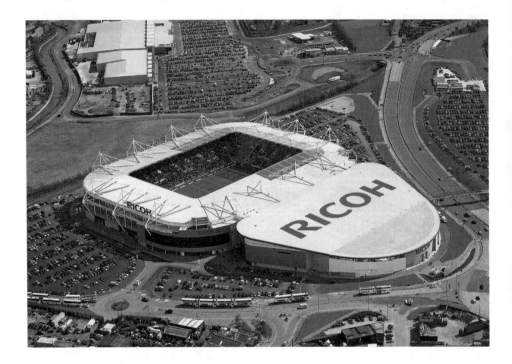

Founded: 1883 (**Entered League**: 1919)
Former Names: Singers FC (1883-1898)
Nickname: 'Sky Blues'
Ground: Ricoh Arena, Phoenix Way, Foleshill,
Coventry   CV6 6GE
Ground Capacity: 32,400 (All seats)
Record Attendance: 51,455 (At Highfield Road)
Pitch Size: 110 × 74 yards

Colours: Sky Blue shirts and socks, White shorts
Telephone Nº: 0844 873-1883
Ticket Office: 0844 873-1883
Fax Numbers: 0844 873-6301 (General Office)
Web Site: www.ccfc.co.uk
E-mail: customer.services@ccfc.co.uk

GENERAL INFORMATION

Car Parking: 2,000 spaces available at the ground. Please pre-book parking via www.ricoharena.com or the ticket office
Coach Parking: At the ground (Car Park 'C')
Nearest Railway Station: Coventry (3 miles)
Nearest Bus Station: Coventry (3 miles)
Club Shop: At the ground and in the City Centre
Opening Times: Weekday office hours and Matchdays
Telephone Nº: 0844 873-1883 (Option 2)

GROUND INFORMATION

Away Supporters' Entrances & Sections:
Turnstiles 1-11

ADMISSION INFO (2012/2013 PRICES)

Adult Seating: £18.00 – £20.00
Child Seating: £9.00 – £10.00
Under-7s Seating: £3.00 – £4.00 (free in the Family Zone)
Concessionary Seating: £12.00 – £14.00
Programme Price: £3.00

DISABLED INFORMATION

Wheelchairs: 94 spaces available
Helpers: Admitted
Prices: Normal prices apply for the disabled. Free for helpers
Disabled Toilets: Available
Contact: 0844 873-1883 Option 2 (Bookings necessary)

Travelling Supporters' Information:
Routes: From All Parts: Exit the M6 at Junction 3 and follow the A444 towards Coventry. The ground is located just 400 yards along this road. Please note that parking spaces at the ground must be pre-booked. No street parking.

CRAWLEY TOWN FC

Founded: 1896 (**Entered League**: 2011)
Former Names: None
Nickname: 'Red Devils'
Ground: Broadfield Stadium, Brighton Road, Crawley, Sussex   RH11 9RX
Record Attendance: 4,516 (2004)
Pitch Size: 110 × 72 yards

Colours: Red shirts and shorts
Telephone Nº: (01293) 410000 (Ground)
Daytime Nº: (01293) 410000 (9.00am – 5.00pm)
Fax Number: (01293) 410002
Ground Capacity: 4,941   **Seating Capacity**: 1,150
Web site: www.crawleytownfc.com
E-mail: customercare@crawleytownfc.com

GENERAL INFORMATION

Supporters Alliance: Ron Parsons, 60 West Street, Southgate, Crawley   RH11 8AW
Telephone Nº: (01293) 430753
Car Parking: 350 spaces available at the ground
Coach Parking: At the ground
Nearest Railway Station: Crawley (1 mile)
Nearest Bus Station: By the Railway Station
Club Shop: At the ground
Opening Times: Weekdays 9.00am to 5.00pm; Saturday matches 12.00pm to 6.00pm; Mid-week matches 6.00pm to kick-off then one hour after the game
Telephone Nº: (01293) 410000

GROUND INFORMATION

Away Supporters' Entrances & Sections:
North Entrance for both terrace and seating

ADMISSION INFO (2012/2013 PRICES)

Adult Standing: £17.00
Adult Seating: £19.00 – £22.00
Under-19s Standing: £7.00
Under-19s Seating: £10.00 – £13.00
Senior Citizen Standing: £13.00
Senior Citizen Seating: £15.00 – £18.00
Programme Price: £2.50

DISABLED INFORMATION

Wheelchairs: Accommodated in the disabled section of the Main Stand (Lift access available)
Helpers: One helper admitted per disabled fan
Prices: Normal prices apply
Disabled Toilets: Available
Contact: (01293) 410000   (Bookings are necessary)

Travelling Supporters' Information:
Routes: Exit the M23 at Junction 11 and take the A23 towards Crawley. After ¼ mile, the Stadium is on the left. Take the first exit at the roundabout for the Stadium entrance.

CREWE ALEXANDRA FC

Founded: 1877 (**Entered League**: 1892)
Nickname: 'Railwaymen'
Ground: Alexandra Stadium, Gresty Road, Crewe, Cheshire   CW2 6EB
Ground Capacity: 10,107 (All seats)
Record Attendance: 20,000 (30th January 1960)
Pitch Size: 112 × 74 yards

Colours: Red shirts with White shorts
Telephone Nº: (01270) 213014
Ticket Office: (01270) 252610
Fax Number: (01270) 216320
Web Site: www.crewealex.net
E-mail: info@crewealex.net

GENERAL INFORMATION

Car Parking: Car Park at the ground (spaces for 400 cars)
Coach Parking: Car Park at the ground
Nearest Railway Station: Crewe (5 minutes walk)
Nearest Bus Station: Crewe Town
Club Shop: At the ground
Opening Times: Monday to Friday and Matchdays 9.00am – 5.00pm (until 7.45pm for Night matches)
Telephone Nº: (01270) 213014 extension 101

GROUND INFORMATION

Away Supporters' Entrances & Sections:
Popular Side Away Stand

ADMISSION INFO (2012/2013 PRICES)

Adult Seating: £16.50 – £19.50
Senior Citizen Seating: £13.00 – £15.50
Under-17s Seating: £7.00 – £9.00
Under-12s Seating: £4.00 – £5.00
Note: Members qualify for the cheaper prices shown.
Programme Price: £2.50

DISABLED INFORMATION

Wheelchairs: Over 70 spaces available in total for home and away fans around the ground
Helpers: One helper admitted per disabled person
Prices: £13.00 – £15.50 for each disabled fan and helper
Disabled Toilets: Available in all Stands
Commentaries are available for the blind
Contact: (01270) 252610   (Bookings are necessary)

Travelling Supporters' Information:
Routes: From the North: Exit the M6 at Junction 17 and take the Crewe (A534) road, and at Crewe roundabout follow signs for Chester into Nantwich Road. Then take a left turn into Gresty Road; From the South and East: Take the A52 to the A5020, then on to Crewe roundabout (then as from the North); From the West: Take the A534 into Crewe and turn right just before the railway station into Gresty Road.

CRYSTAL PALACE FC

Founded: 1905 (**Entered League**: 1920)
Nickname: 'Eagles'
Ground: Selhurst Park, London   SE25 6PU
Ground Capacity: 26,247 (All seats)
Record Attendance: 51,482 (11th May 1979)
Pitch Size: 110 × 74 yards

Colours: Red and Blue striped shirts with Blue shorts
Telephone Nº: (020) 8768-6000
Ticket Office: 0871 200-0071
Fax Number: (020) 8771-5311
Web Site: www.cpfc.co.uk
E-mail: communications@cpfc.co.uk

GENERAL INFORMATION
Car Parking: Street Parking only
Coach Parking: Thornton Heath
Nearest Railway Station: Selhurst or Norwood Junction
(both 5 minutes walk)
Nearest Bus Station: West Croydon
Club Shop: At the ground
Opening Times: Weekdays & Matchdays 9.00am to 6.00pm
Telephone Nº: (020) 8768-6100

GROUND INFORMATION
Away Supporters' Entrances & Sections:
Park Road for the Arthur Wait Stand

ADMISSION INFO (2011/2012 PRICES)
Adult Seating: £25.00 – £30.00
Concessionary Seating: £15.00 – £18.00
Under-16s Seating: £5.00 – £10.00
Programme Price: £3.00

DISABLED INFORMATION
Wheelchairs: Spaces are available in the disabled area,
Holmesdale Road Stand and also in the Arthur Wait Stand
Helpers: One helper admitted per wheelchair
Prices: Normal prices apply for the disabled. Helpers are
admitted free of charge
Disabled Toilets: Located in the disabled section
Commentaries are available for 12 people
Contact: (020) 8768-6080   (Bookings are necessary)

Travelling Supporters' Information:
Routes: From the North: Take the M1/A1 to the North Circular (A406) for Chiswick. Take the South Circular (A205) to Wandsworth then the A3 to the A214 and follow signs for Streatham to the A23. Turn left onto the B273 after 1 mile, follow to the end, turn left into the High Street and then into Whitehorse Lane; From the East: Take the A232 (Croydon Road) to Shirley and join the A215 (Northwood Road). After 2¼ miles turn left into Whitehorse Lane; From the South: Take the A23 and follow signs for Crystal Palace (B266) through Thornton Heath into Whitehorse Lane; From the West: Take the M4 to Chiswick (then as North).

DAGENHAM & REDBRIDGE FC

Founded: 1992   (**Entered League**: 2007)
Former Names: Formed by the merger of
Dagenham FC and Redbridge Forest FC
Nickname: 'The Daggers'
Ground: London Borough of Barking and Dagenham
Stadium, Victoria Road, Dagenham   RM10 7XL
Record Attendance: 7,100 (1967)
Pitch Size: 110 × 65 yards

Colours: Red and Blue shirts with Blue shorts
Telephone N°: (020) 8592-1549
Office Phone N°: (020) 8592-7194
Secretary's Phone N°: (020) 8592-1549
Fax Number: (020) 8593-7227
Ground Capacity: 6,078 **Seating Capacity**: 2,233
Web site: www.daggers.co.uk
E-mail: info@daggers.co.uk

GENERAL INFORMATION

Car Parking: Street parking only
Coach Parking: Street parking only
Nearest Railway Station: Dagenham East (5 mins. walk)
Nearest Bus Station: Romford
Club Shop: At the ground
Opening Times: Monday & Tuesday 12.00pm – 4.00pm;
Thursday 12.00pm – 8.00pm; Friday 12.00pm – 6.00pm;
Saturday matchdays 1.00pm – 3.00pm.
Closed on Wednesdays, Sundays and non-match Saturdays
Telephone N°: (020) 8592-7194

GROUND INFORMATION

Away Supporters' Entrances & Sections:
Pondfield Road entrances for Pondfield Road End

ADMISSION INFO (2012/2013 PRICES)

Adult Standing: £15.00 – £17.00
Adult Seating: £16.00 – £22.00
Concessionary Standing: £10.00 – £11.00
Concessionary Seating: £13.00 – £15.00
Under-18s Standing: £6.00 – £11.00
Under-18s Seating: £7.00 in the Family Stand
Note: Discounts are available for tickets bought before the day
of the game and also for home fans in the Family Area
Programme Price: £2.50

DISABLED INFORMATION

Wheelchairs: Accommodated in front of the new Stand
and the Barking College Stand
Helpers: Admitted
Prices: £10.00 for the disabled. Free of charge for Helpers
Disabled Toilets: Available at the East and West ends of the
ground and also in the Clubhouse
Contact: (020) 8592-7194   (Bookings are necessary)

Travelling Supporters' Information:
Routes: From the North & West: Take the M11 to its end and join the A406 South. At the large roundabout take the slip road
on the left signposted A13 to Dagenham. As you approach Dagenham, stay in the left lane and follow signs for A1306 signposted
Dagenham East. Turn left onto the A1112 at the 3rd set of traffic lights by the McDonalds. Proceed along Ballards Road to The
Bull roundabout and bear left. Victoria Road is 450 yards on the left after passing Dagenham East tube station; From the South
& East: Follow signs for the A13 to Dagenham. Take the next slip road off signposted Elm Park & Dagenham East then turn right
at the roundabout. Go straight on at the next roundabout and turn left onto A1306. After ½ mile you will see a McDonalds on
the right. Get into the right hand filter lane and turn right onto A1112. Then as from the North & West.

DERBY COUNTY FC

Founded: 1884 (**Entered League**: 1888)
Nickname: 'Rams'
Ground: Pride Park Stadium, Royal Way, Pride Park, Derby DE24 8XL
Ground Capacity: 33,455 (All seats)
Record Attendance: 33,597 (25th May 2001)
Pitch Size: 110 × 74 yards

Colours: White shirts with Black shorts
Telephone Nº: 0871 472-1884
Ticket Office: 0871 472-1884
Fax Number: (01332) 667519
Web Site: www.dcfc.co.uk
E-mail: derby.county@dcfc.co.uk

GENERAL INFORMATION

Car Parking: Spaces for 1,424 cars at the ground (available for permit holders only)
Coach Parking: At the ground
Nearest Railway Station: Derby Midland (1 mile)
Nearest Bus Station: Derby Central
Club Shop: shop dcfc at the ground
Opening Times: Monday to Saturday 9.00am – 5.00pm (from 10.00am on Tuesdays); Sundays 10.00am – 4.00pm
Telephone Nº: 0871 472-1884

GROUND INFORMATION

Away Supporters' Entrances & Sections:
South Stand

ADMISSION INFO (2012/2013 PRICES)

For the 2012/2013 season, Derby County are operating a demand-based pricing system so prices will vary depending on the demand for tickets and the date at which they are purchased. Please contact the club for further pricing details about individual games.
Programme Price: £3.00

DISABLED INFORMATION

Wheelchairs: 206 spaces available in total
Helpers: One helper admitted for each disabled fan
Prices: £25.00 – £39.00 for each disabled fan & helper
Disabled Toilets: Yes
Contact: 0871 472-1884 (Bookings are necessary)

Travelling Supporters' Information:
Routes: From All Parts: Exit the M1 at Junction 25 and follow the A52 towards the City Centre until the ground is signposted on the left. Follow the signs for the ground.
From the Train Station: The Stadium is 10 minutes walk by way of a tunnel under the railway opposite Brunswick Inn, Station Approach. Then follow the footpath; Buses: A shuttle service runs from the bus station from 1.00pm until 2.45pm on Saturdays. A similar service runs from 6.00pm – 7.30pm for midweek games. Return shuttles are available post-match.

DONCASTER ROVERS FC

Founded: 1879
Former Names: None
Nickname: 'Rovers'
Ground: Keepmoat Stadium, Stadium Way, Doncaster   DN4 5JW
Record Attendance: 15,001 (1st April 2008)
Pitch Size: 110 × 72 yards

Colours: Red & White hooped shirts with Black shorts
Telephone Nº: (01302) 764664
Ticket Office: (01302) 762576
Fax Number: (01302) 363525
Ground Capacity: 15,231 (All seats)
Web site: www.doncasterroversfc.co.uk
E-mail: info@doncasterroversfc.co.uk

GENERAL INFORMATION
Car Parking: 1,000 spaces available at the ground
Coach Parking: At the ground
Nearest Railway Station: Doncaster (2 miles)
Nearest Bus Station: Doncaster (2 miles)
Club Shop: At the ground
Opening Times: 10.00am to 4.30pm on weekdays and 10.00am to 4.00pm on Saturdays
Telephone Nº: (01302) 764667

GROUND INFORMATION
Away Supporters' Entrances & Sections:
North Stand

ADMISSION INFO (2012/2013 PRICES)
Adult Seating: £20.00 – £23.00
Concessionary Seating: £15.00 – £18.00
Ages 17 to 20 Seating: £11.00 – £13.00
Under-17s Seating: £8.00   **Under-12s Seating**: £5.00
Note: Prices vary depending on the category of the game and discounts are available for tickets bought in advance
Programme Price: £3.00

DISABLED INFORMATION
Wheelchairs: Accommodated throughout the ground (Away fans accommodated in the North Stand)
Helpers: Admitted
Prices: £15.00 – £20.00 for the disabled. Helpers are admitted free of charge
Disabled Toilets: Available in all Stands
Contact: (01302) 764664   (Bookings are necessary)

Travelling Supporters' Information:
Routes: Exit the M18 at Junction 3 and follow the A6182 towards Doncaster. The stadium is approximately 1½ miles from the motorway and is well signposted so follow these signs. There are 1,000 car parking spaces available at the stadium and the cost is £5.00 per car. A number of businesses on the nearby business park also offer matchday parking for a similar charge. When crowds over 9,000 are expected, a Park and Ride service runs from Doncaster Racecourse. The shuttle service buses run from 1.00pm to 3.00pm to the Stadium and from 4.30pm to 6.30pm returning to the Racecourse from the Stadium.

EVERTON FC

Founded: 1878 (**Entered League**: 1888)
Former Names: St. Domingo's FC (1878-79)
Nickname: 'The Toffees'
Ground: Goodison Park, Goodison Road, Liverpool L4 4EL
Ground Capacity: 40,565 (All seats)
Record Attendance: 78,299 (18th September 1948)

Pitch Size: 110 × 74 yards
Colours: Blue shirts with White shorts
Telephone Nº: 0870 442-1878
Ticket Office: 0870 442-1878
Fax Number: (0151) 286-9112
Web Site: www.evertonfc.com
E-mail: everton@evertonfc.com

GENERAL INFORMATION

Car Parking: Corner of Priory Road and Utting Avenue
Coach Parking: Priory Road
Nearest Railway Station: Kirkdale
Nearest Mainline Railway Station: Liverpool Lime Street
Nearest Bus Station: Queen's Square, Liverpool
Club Shop: 'Megastore' in Walton Lane by the ground
Opening Times: Weekdays 9.30am to 5.00pm, Wednesdays 10.00am to 5.00pm. Saturdays 9.00am to 5.00pm. Open one hour after matches
Telephone Nº: 0870 442-1878

GROUND INFORMATION

Away Supporters' Entrances & Sections:
Bullens Road entrances for Bullens Stand

ADMISSION INFO (2012/2013 PRICES)

Adult Seating: £31.00 – £43.00
Junior Seating: £15.50 – £21.50
Senior Citizen Seating: £21.25 – £27.50
Note: Concessionary prices are only available in some areas and prices vary depending on the category of the game
Programme Price: £3.00

DISABLED INFORMATION

Wheelchairs: 85 spaces for home fans, 13 spaces for away fans in the disabled section.
Helpers: One helper admitted per wheelchair
Prices: £25.00 for each disabled fan + 1 helper
Disabled Toilets: Available in the disabled section
Commentaries are available for the blind
Contact: 0870 442-1878   (Bookings are necessary)

Travelling Supporters' Information:
Routes: From the North: Exit the M6 at Junction 26 onto the M58 and continue to it's end. Take the 2nd exit at the roundabout onto the A59 Ormskirk Road. Continue along into Rice Lane and go straight across at the next roundabout into County Road. After ½ mile, turn left into Everton Valley then bear left into Walton Lane for the ground; From the South & East: Exit the M6 at Junction 21A and take the M62 to it's end. Turn right at traffic lights onto A5088 Queen Drive and continue to the junction with Walton Hall Avenue then turn left into Walton Lane (A580) and the ground is on the right.
Bus Services: Services to the ground – 19, 20, F1, F2, 30

EXETER CITY FC

Founded: 1904   (**Re-Entered League**: 2008)
Former Names: Formed by the amalgamation of
St. Sidwell United FC & Exeter United FC
Nickname: 'Grecians'
Ground: St. James Park, Exeter, EX4 6PX
Ground Capacity: 8,677
Seating Capacity: 3,806
Record Attendance: 20,984 (4th March 1931)

Pitch Size: 113 × 71 yards
Colours: Red and White striped shirts, Black shorts
Telephone Nº: (01392) 411243
Ticket Office: (01392) 411243
or 08448 444410 (Advance Home ticket sales)
Fax Number: (01392) 413959
Web Site: www.exetercityfc.co.uk
E-mail: reception@exetercityfc.co.uk

GENERAL INFORMATION

Car Parking: King William Street and Western Way car parks
Coach Parking: Paris Street Bus Station
Nearest Railway Station: Exeter St. James Park (adjacent)
Nearest Bus Station: Paris Street Bus Station
Club Shop: At the ground
Opening Times: Monday to Saturday 11.00am to 5.00pm
but closed on Wednesdays
Club Shop Telephone Nº: (01392) 425885

GROUND INFORMATION

Away Supporters' Entrances & Sections:
St. James Road turnstiles for standing in the St. James Road
End and access to seating in the Stagecoach Family Stand

ADMISSION INFO (2012/2013 PRICES)

Adult Standing: £17.00
Adult Seating: £21.00 – £24.00
Concessionary Standing: £12.00
Concessionary Seating: £15.00 – £19.00
Under-18s Standing: £5.00   **Seating**: £6.00 – £15.00
Under-12s Standing: £2.00   **Seating**: £2.00 – £5.00
Note: The Under-12s seating prices shown are not available
in some areas of the ground.
Programme Price: £3.00

DISABLED INFORMATION

Wheelchairs: Accommodated in the Flybe Stand and Big
Bank Stand
Helpers: One assistant admitted per wheelchair
Prices: Free of charge for assistants. Normal prices apply for
the disabled
Disabled Toilets: Available by the Big Bank Stand
Contact: (01392) 411243   (Bookings are necessary)

Travelling Supporters' Information:
Routes: From the North: Exit the M5 at Junction 29 and follow signs to the City Centre along Heavitree Road. Take the 4th exit
at the roundabout into Western Way and the 2nd exit into Tiverton Road then 2nd left into Stadium Way; From the East: Take
the A30 into Heavitree Road (then as from the North); From the South & West: Take the A38 and follow City Centre signs into
Western Way, then take the third exit at the roundabout into St. James Road.
Note: This ground is very difficult to find being in a residential area on the side of a hill without prominent floodlights.

FLEETWOOD TOWN FC

Founded: 1977   (**Entered League**: 2012)
Former Names: None (The club succeeded Fleetwood FC who existed from 1907-1977)
Nickname: 'The Fishermen'
Ground: Highbury Stadium, Park Avenue, Fleetwood FY7 6TX
Record Attendance: 6,150 vs Rochdale FC (1965)
Pitch Size: 112 × 71 yards

Colours: Red shirts with White sleeves, White shorts
Telephone Nº: (01253) 770702
Fax Number: (01253) 770702
Ground Capacity: 3,450
Seating Capacity: 550
Web site: www.fleetwoodtownfc.com
E-mail: info@fleetwoodtownfc.com

GENERAL INFORMATION

Car Parking: Spaces for 40 cars at the ground and also street parking
Coach Parking: At the ground
Nearest Railway Station: Poulton (7 miles)
Nearest Bus Station: Fleetwood
Club Shop: Sales via the club web site only
Opening Times: None
Telephone Nº: –

GROUND INFORMATION

Away Supporters' Entrances & Sections:
No usual segregation

ADMISSION INFO (2012/2013 PRICES)

Adult Standing: £12.50 – £15.00
Adult Seating: £14.00 – £17.00
Under-16s Standing: £5.00 – £7.00   (Under-5s admitted
Under-16s Seating: £6.00 – £9.00   free of charge)
Senior Citizen Standing: £8.00 – £10.00
Senior Citizen Seating: £9.00 – £12.00
Note: Discounts are available for tickets purchased in advance
Programme Price: £2.50

DISABLED INFORMATION

Wheelchairs: Accommodated
Helpers: Admitted
Prices: Normal prices apply for the disabled and helpers
Disabled Toilets: Available
Contact: (01253) 770702   (Bookings are necessary)

Travelling Supporters' Information:
Routes: Exit the M55 at Junction 3 and take the A585 to Fleetwood (approximately 11½ miles). Upon reaching Fleetwood, take the 1st exit at the Nautical College roundabout (with the statue of Eros in the middle) and continue for about 1 mile to the next roundabout. Take the 6th exit onto Hatfield Avenue and after about ½ mile (when the road bends to the right)m turn left into Nelson Road. The ground is situated on the left after 100 yards.

FULHAM FC

Founded: 1879 (**Entered League**: 1907)
Former Names: Fulham St. Andrew's FC (1879-1898)
Nickname: 'The Whites'
Ground: Craven Cottage, Stevenage Road, Fulham, London   SW6 6HH
Ground Capacity: 25,700 (All seats)
Record Attendance: 49,335 (8th October 1938)

Pitch Size: 109 × 71 yards
Colours: White shirts with Black shorts
Telephone Nº: 0843 208-1222
Ticket Office: 0843 208-1234
Fax Number: (020) 7384-4810
Web Site: www.fulhamfc.com
E-mail: enquiries@fulhamfc.com

GENERAL INFORMATION

Car Parking: Street Parking (Matchday restrictions apply)
Coach Parking: Stevenage Road/Fulham Palace Road
Nearest Railway Station: Putney (1 mile)
Nearest Tube Station: Putney Bridge (District) (1 mile)
Club Shop: At the ground and Fulham Road
Opening Times: At the ground: Monday to Friday 9.00am to 5.00pm; Fulham Road: Monday to Saturday 9.00am to 5.00pm and Sundays 11.00am to 3.00pm
Telephone Nº: 0870 442-1223

GROUND INFORMATION

Away Supporters' Entrances & Sections:
Putney End for the Putney Stand

ADMISSION INFO (2012/2013 PRICES)

Adult Seating: £30.00 – £75.00
Child Seating: £10.00 – £55.00 (£1.00 for certain games)
Concessionary Seating: £20.00 – £65.00
Note: Prices vary depending on the category of the game.
Programme Price: £3.50

DISABLED INFORMATION

Wheelchairs: 31 spaces for Home fans and 9 spaces for Away fans in the Putney End, Block 7
Helpers: One assistant admitted per disabled person
Prices: Half-price for the disabled. Free of charge for assistants
Disabled Toilets: Available next to each disabled area
Contact: 0843 208-1234 (Bookings necessary)

Travelling Supporters' Information:
Routes: From the North: Take the A1/M1 to the North Circular (A406), travel west to Neasden and follow signs for Harlesdon A404, then Hammersmith A219. At Broadway, follow the Fulham sign and turn right after 1 mile into Harboard Street then left at the end for the ground; From the South & East: Take the South Circular (A205), follow the Putney Bridge sign (A219). Cross the bridge and follow Hammersmith signs for ½ mile, turn left into Bishops Park Road, then right at the end; From the West: Take the M4 to the A4. Branch left after 2 miles into Hammersmith Broadway (then as from the North).

GILLINGHAM FC

Founded: 1893 (**Entered League**: 1920)
Former Names: New Brompton FC (1893-1913)
Nickname: 'Gills'
Ground: Priestfield Stadium, Redfern Avenue, Gillingham, Kent   ME7 4DD
Ground Capacity: 11,440 (All seats)
Record Attendance: 23,002 (10th January 1948)

Pitch Size: 114 × 75 yards
Telephone Nº: (01634) 300000
Ticket Office: (01634) 300000 Option 1
Fax Number: (01634) 850986
Web Site: www.gillinghamfootballclub.com
E-mail: enquiries@priestfield.com

GENERAL INFORMATION
Car Parking: Street parking
Coach Parking: By Police direction
Nearest Railway Station: Gillingham
Nearest Bus Station: Gillingham
Club Shop: Megastore in Redfern Avenue
Opening Times: Megastore is open Weekdays and Matchdays from 9.00am to 5.00pm
Telephone Nº: (01634) 300000

GROUND INFORMATION
Away Supporters' Entrances & Sections:
Priestfield Road End

ADMISSION INFO (2012/2013 PRICES)
Adult Seating: £20.00 – £26.00
Senior Citizen Seating: £19.00
Under-22s Seating: £16.00
Under-16s Seating: £11.00
Under-11s Seating: £7.00
Note: Discounted prices are available for tickets purchased prior to the matchday (matchday prices shown above)
Programme Price: £3.00

DISABLED INFORMATION
Wheelchairs: 65 spaces in total for Home and Away fans and helpers in disabled sections around the ground
Helpers: One helper admitted per disabled person
Prices: Normal prices for the disabled. Free for helpers
Disabled Toilets: Available in the Gordon Road Stand
Contact: (01634) 300000   (Bookings are necessary)

Travelling Supporters' Information:
Routes: From All Parts: Exit the M2 at Junction 4 and follow the link road (dual carriageway) B278 to the 3rd roundabout. Turn left onto the A2 (dual carriageway) and go across the roundabout to the traffic lights. Turn right into Woodlands Road after the traffic lights. The ground is ¼ mile on the left.

HARTLEPOOL UNITED FC

Founded: 1908 (**Entered League**: 1921)
Former Names: Hartlepools United FC (1908-68); Hartlepool FC (1968-77)
Nickname: 'The Pool' 'Pools'
Ground: Victoria Park, Clarence Road, Hartlepool, TS24 8BZ
Ground Capacity: 7,856 **Seating Capacity**: 4,249
Record Attendance: 17,426 (15th January 1957)

Pitch Size: 110 × 74 yards
Colours: Blue and White striped shirts with Blue shorts
Telephone Nº: (01429) 272584
Ticket Office: (01429) 272584 Extension 2
Ticket Office e-mail: tickets@hartlepoolunited.co.uk
Fax Number: (01429) 863007
Web Site: www.hartlepoolunited.co.uk
E-mail: enquiries@hartlepoolunited.co.uk

GENERAL INFORMATION

Car Parking: Limited space at the ground (£8.00 charge) and also street parking
Coach Parking: Church Street
Nearest Railway Station: Hartlepool Church Street (5 minutes walk)
Club Shop: At the ground
Opening Times: Weekdays 9.00am to 5.00pm; non-match Saturdays 9.00am to 1.00pm. Saturday matchdays 10.00am–3.00pm and 4.30pm–5.30pm
Telephone Nº: (01429) 260491

GROUND INFORMATION

Away Supporters' Entrances & Sections:
Clarence Road turnstiles 1 & 2 for Smith & Graham Stand

ADMISSION INFO (2012/2013 PRICES)

Adult Standing: £20.00
Adult Seating: £25.00
Child/Senior Citizen Standing: £10.00
Child/Senior Citizen Seating: £13.00
Programme Price: £3.00

DISABLED INFORMATION

Wheelchairs: 21 spaces for Home fans in disabled section, Cyril Knowles Stand, 10 spaces for Away fans in the Smith & Graham Stand.
Helpers: One helper admitted per wheelchair
Prices: £25.00 for the Disabled. Helpers free of charge
Disabled Toilets: Available in the Cyril Knowles Stand
Contact: (01429) 272584   (Bookings are advisable)

Travelling Supporters' Information: **Routes**: From the North: Take the A1/A19 to the A179 and follow Town Centre/Marina signs. Turn right at the roundabout by the 'Historic Quayside' and cross over the Railway bridge. The ground is on the left; From the South & West: Take the A689 following Town Centre/Marina signs. Turn left at the roundabout by the 'Historic Quayside' and cross over the Railway bridge. The ground is on the left.

HUDDERSFIELD TOWN FC |

Founded: 1908 (**Entered League**: 1910)
Nickname: 'Terriers'
Ground: The Galpharm Stadium, Huddersfield, HD1 6PX
Ground Capacity: 24,554 (All seats)
Record Attendance: 23,678 (12th December 1999)
Pitch Size: 115 × 76 yards

Colours: Blue and White striped shirts, Blue shorts and White socks
Telephone N°: 0870 444-4677
Ticket Office: (01484) 484123
Fax Number: (01484) 484101
Web Site: www.htafc.com
E-mail: info@htafc.com

GENERAL INFORMATION

Car Parking: Car park for 1,100 cars adjacent (pre-sold)
Coach Parking: Adjacent car park
Nearest Railway Station: Huddersfield (1¼ miles)
Nearest Bus Station: Huddersfield
Club Shop: At the ground and in the Town Centre
Opening Times: Weekdays 9.00am to 5.00pm, Saturday Matchdays 9.00am to 3.00pm and Saturday Non-matchdays 9.00am to 12.00pm
Telephone N°:. (01484) 484144 or 421612

GROUND INFORMATION

Away Supporters' Entrances & Sections:
Pink Link Stand

ADMISSION INFO (2011/2012 PRICES)

Adult Seating: £19.00 – £28.00
Under-16s Seating: £5.00 – £12.00
Senior Citizen/Student Seating: £10.00 – £20.00
Programme Price: £3.00

DISABLED INFORMATION

Wheelchairs: 254 spaces in total for home and away fans in the disabled sections, Direct Golf UK Lower Stand, Pink Link Stand and Antich Stand. Additional spaces are available for the ambulant disabled and visually impaired.
Helpers: Admitted
Prices: £11.00 – £28.00 for the disabled. Free of charge for helpers
Disabled Toilets: Available in the disabled sections Commentaries are available for the blind.
Contact: (01484) 484123   (Bookings are necessary)

Travelling Supporters' Information:
Routes: From the North, East and West: Exit the M62 at Junction 25 and take the A644 and A62 following Huddersfield signs. Follow signs for the Galpharm Stadium; From the South: Leave the M1 at Junction 38 and follow the A637/A642 to Huddersfield. At the Ring Road, follow signs for the A62 to the Galpharm Stadium.

HULL CITY AFC

Founded: 1904 (**Entered League**: 1905)
Nickname: 'Tigers'
Ground: KC Stadium, The Circle, Walton Street, Hull   HU3 6HU
Ground Capacity: 25,466 (All seats)
Record Attendance: 24,945 (24th May 2009)
Pitch Size: 115 × 75 yards

Colours: Black and Amber shirts with Black shorts
Telephone Nº: (01482) 504600
Ticket Office: (01482) 505600
Fax Number: (01482) 304882
Web Site: www.hullcityafc.net
E-mail: info@hulltigers.com

GENERAL INFORMATION

Car Parking: Walton Street Car Park (£5.00), City Centre Car Parks and a Park & Ride scheme from Priory Park (£1.20)
Coach Parking: By Police direction
Nearest Railway Station: Hull Interchange
Nearest Bus Station: City Centre, Hull
Club Shop: Tiger Leisure Superstore at the Stadium
Opening Times: Monday to Saturday 9.00am to 5.00pm. Open until 5.30pm on Saturday matchdays
Telephone Nº: (01482) 509600

GROUND INFORMATION

Away Supporters' Entrances & Sections: North Stand

ADMISSION INFO (2011/2012 PRICES)

Adult Seating: £21.00 – £27.50
Concessionary Seating: £13.00 – £17.00
Child Seating: £3.00 – £15.00 (Price depends on child's age)
Note: Prices vary depending on the category of the game
Programme Price: £3.00

DISABLED INFORMATION

Wheelchairs: 304 spaces in total for Home and Away fans available around all the stands at both upper and lower level
Helpers: One helper admitted per disabled person (subject to registration)
Prices: Concessionary rates for the disabled. Free for helpers
Disabled Toilets: Many available throughout the ground. Lifts are available. Commentaries are available for the blind
Contact: (01482) 504600   (Bookings are not necessary)

Travelling Supporters' Information:
Routes: From the West: Take the M62 then join the A63. Continue under the Humber Bridge as the road becomes the A63 Clive Sullivan Way and turn off at the slip road just before the flyover marked "Local Traffic/Infirmary". Take the 2nd exit at the roundabout into Rawling Way. Turn left at the next main set of traffic lights on A1105 Anlaby Road. Continue over the flyover then take a right turn into Walton Street. The car park is half way down this street after the Sports Arena; From the Humber Bridge: Follow signs for Hull City Centre – the road curves round to the left to join the A63 Clive Sullivan Way. Then as from the West; From the North: Take the A1079 towards Beverley then follow signs for the Humber Bridge and A164. Take the A63 sign-posted Hull City Centre and follow onto the A63 Clive Sullivan Way. Then as from the West.

IPSWICH TOWN FC

Founded: 1878 (**Entered League**: 1938)
Nickname: 'Town' 'Tractor Boys'
Ground: Portman Road, Ipswich IP1 2DA
Ground Capacity: 30,311 (All seats)
Record Attendance: 38,010 (8th March 1975)
Pitch Size: 110 × 72 yards

Colours: Blue shirts with White shorts
Telephone N°: (01473) 400500
Ticket Office: 0870 111-0555
Fax Number: (01473) 400040
Web Site: www.itfc.co.uk
E-mail: enquiries@itfc.co.uk

GENERAL INFORMATION

Car Parking: Portman Road & Sir Alf Ramsey Way car parks
Coach Parking: Bibb Way
Nearest Railway Station: Ipswich (5 minutes walk)
Nearest Bus Station: Ipswich
Club Shop: At the ground
Opening Times: Weekdays 8.30am–5.00pm. Opening times on Matchdays vary. Please contact the club for details
Telephone N°: (01473) 400501

GROUND INFORMATION

Away Supporters' Entrances & Sections:
Cobbold Stand

ADMISSION INFO (2011/2012 PRICES)

Adult Seating: £27.50 – £59.50
Child Seating: £8.50 – £29.50
Senior Citizen Seating: £19.00 – £45.50
Note: Discounts are available for advance ticket purchases.
Programme Price: £3.00

DISABLED INFORMATION

Wheelchairs: 103 spaces and 103 seats for home fans in the Britannia, South and North Stands upper and lower tiers. 10 spaces and 10 seats for away fans in the lower Britannia Stand only.
Helpers: One helper admitted per disabled person
Prices: Adult price charged for disabled fan + one helper.
Disabled Toilets: Adjacent to the disabled areas
Commentaries are available for the blind
Contact: 0870 111-0555 (Bookings are necessary)

Travelling Supporters' Information:
Routes: From the North and West: Take the A1214 from the A14/A12 following signs for Ipswich West only. Proceed through Holiday Inn Hotel traffic lights and at the 3rd set of traffic lights turn right into West End Road. The ground is ¼ mile along on the left; From the South: Follow signs for Ipswich West, then as from the North and West above.

LEEDS UNITED FC

Founded: 1919 (**Entered League**: 1920)
Former Names: Formed after Leeds City FC were wound up for 'Irregular Practices'
Nickname: 'United'
Ground: Elland Road, Leeds LS11 0ES
Ground Capacity: 39,460 (All seats)
Record Attendance: 57,892 (15th March 1967)

Pitch Size: 115 × 74 yards
Colours: White shirts and shorts
Telephone N°: 0871 334-1919
Ticket Office: 0871 334-1992
Fax Number: (0113) 367-6050
Web Site: www.leedsunited.com
E-mail: reception@leedsunited.com

GENERAL INFORMATION
Car Parking: Large car parks adjacent to the Stadium
Coach Parking: Adjacent to the Stadium
Nearest Railway Station: Leeds City (1½ miles)
Nearest Bus Station: Leeds City Centre – specials from Swinegate
Club Shop: At the South East corner of the Stadium
Opening Times: Weekdays 9.00am to 5.00pm, Matchdays 9.00am to one hour after the final whistle
Telephone N°: (0113) 367-6221

GROUND INFORMATION
Away Supporters' Entrances & Sections:
South East Corner or South Stand – Upper & Lower Tiers

ADMISSION INFO (2012/2013 PRICES)
Adult Seating: £19.00 – £35.00
Child Seating: £11.00 – £16.00 (£11.00 in Family Stand)
Senior Citizen Seating: £15.00 – £20.00
Note: Prices vary according to the category of game played.
Programme Price: £3.00

DISABLED INFORMATION
Wheelchairs: 131 spaces in total in the disabled sections, West, North and South Stands
Helpers: One helper admitted per disabled person
Prices: Please contact the club for details
Disabled Toilets: Adjacent to each of the disabled sections
Commentaries via headphones in the West Stand
Contact: (0113) 367-6178 (Ms. Tracey Lazenby)
(Bookings are necessary)

Travelling Supporters' Information:
Routes: From the North: Take the A58 or A61 into the City Centre and follow signs to the M621. Leave the Motorway after 1½ miles and exit the roundabout onto the A643 into Elland Road; From the North-East: Take the A63 or A64 into the City Centre (then as from the North); From the South: Take the M1 to the M621 (then as from the North); From the West: Take the M62 to the M621 (then as from the North).

LEICESTER CITY FC

Founded: 1884 (**Entered League**: 1894)
Former Names: Leicester Fosse FC (1884-1919)
Nickname: 'Foxes'
Ground: Walkers Stadium, Filbert Way, Leicester, LE2 7FL
Ground Capacity: 32,500 (All seats)
Record Attendance: 32,148 (26th December 2003)

Pitch Size: 110 × 72 yards
Colours: Blue shirts with White shorts
Telephone Nº: 0844 815-6000
Ticket Office: 0844 815-5000
Fax Number: (0116) 229-4404
Web Site: www.lcfc.com

GENERAL INFORMATION

Car Parking: NCP Car Park (5 minutes walk)
Coach Parking: Sawday Street
Nearest Railway Station: Leicester (1 mile)
Nearest Bus Station: St. Margaret's (1 mile)
Club Shop: At the ground
Opening Times: Monday to Saturday 9.00am–5.00pm. Saturday Matchdays open 9.00am until kick-off then for 30 minutes after the game. Sundays open 10.00am – 4.00pm
Telephone Nº: 0844 815-6000

GROUND INFORMATION

Away Supporters' Entrances & Sections:
At the corner of the North and East Stands

ADMISSION INFO (2011/2012 PRICES)

Adult Seating: £20.00 – £40.00
Under-8s Seating: £5.00 – £12.00 (Free in North Stand)
Under-18s Seating: £11.00 – £26.00
Under-22s Seating: £13.00 – £30.00
Senior Citizen Seating: £17.00 – £34.00
Note: Various discounts are available for members
Programme Price: £3.00

DISABLED INFORMATION

Wheelchairs: 186 spaces for the disabled + 111 spaces for helpers accommodated at various levels in all stands
Helpers: One carer admitted per disabled person
Prices: Reduced prices are available – Phone for details
Disabled Toilets: Available in all stands
Contact: 0844 815-5000 (Hayley Mason – phone or fax)

Travelling Supporters' Information:
Routes: From the North: Take the A46/A607 into the City Centre or exit the M1 at Junction 21, take the A5460, turn right ¾ mile after the Railway Bridge into Upperton Road, then right into Filbert Way; From the East: Take the A47 into the City Centre (then as from the North); From the South: Exit the M1 at Junction 21 and take the A5460, turn right ¾ mile after Railway Bridge into Upperton Road, then right into Filbert Way; From the West: Take the M69 to the City Centre (then as from North).

LEYTON ORIENT FC

Founded: 1881 (**Entered League**: 1905)
Former Names: Glyn Cricket and Football Club
(1881-86); Eagle FC (1886-88); Clapton Orient FC
(1888-1946); Leyton Orient FC (1946-66); Orient FC
(1966-87)
Nickname: 'O's'
Ground: Matchroom Stadium, Brisbane Road,
Leyton, London   E10 5NF

Ground Capacity: 9,311 (all seats)
Record Attendance: 34,345 (21st January 1964)
Pitch Size: 110 × 76 yards
Telephone Nº: 0871 310-1881
Ticket Office: 0871 310-1883
Fax Number: 0871 310-1882
Web Site: www.leytonorient.com

GENERAL INFORMATION
Car Parking: Street parking
Coach Parking: By Police direction
Nearest Railway Station: Leyton Midland Road (½ mile)
Nearest Tube Station: Leyton (Central)
Club Shop: At the ground
Opening Times: Weekdays 9.30am to 4.30pm
Telephone Nº: 0871 310-1889

GROUND INFORMATION
Away Supporters' Entrances & Sections:
East Stand

ADMISSION INFO (2012/2013 PRICES)
Adult Seating: £23.00 – £40.00
Child Seating: £5.00 in the North Family Stand only – free
of charge for Under-11s if booked in advance
Senior Citizen Seating: £14.00 – £30.00
Note: Tickets are cheaper when purchased in advance
Programme Price: £3.00

DISABLED INFORMATION
Wheelchairs: Spaces are available in the North, East and
West Stands
Helpers: One helper admitted per disabled person
Prices: Free of charge for the disabled and helpers
Disabled Toilets: Available near disabled sections
Contact: 0871 310-1883   (Bookings are necessary)

Travelling Supporters' Information:
Routes: From the North & West: Take A406 North Circular, follow signs for Chelmsford to Edmonton. After 2½ miles take the
3rd exit at the roundabout towards Leyton (A112). Pass the railway station, turn right after ½ mile into Windsor Road and left
into Brisbane Road; From the East: Follow the A12 to London then the City for Leytonstone. Follow Hackney signs into Grove
Road, cross Main Road into Ruckholt Road then turn right into Leyton High Road, turn left after ¼ mile into Buckingham Road
and left into Brisbane Road; From the South: Take the A102M through the Blackwall Tunnel, follow signs for Newmarket (A102)
to join the A11 to Stratford, then follow signs for Stratford Station into Leyton Road to the railway station (then as from North).

LIVERPOOL FC

Founded: 1892 (**Entered League**: 1893)	**Colours**: Red shirts, shorts and socks
Nickname: 'Reds'	**Telephone Nº**: (0151) 263-2361
Ground: Anfield Road, Liverpool L4 0TH	**Ticket Office**: 0843 170-5555
Ground Capacity: 45,362 (All seats)	**Ticket Office Fax Number**: (0151) 261-1416
Record Attendance: 61,905 (2nd February 1952)	**Customer Services**: 0843 170-5000
Pitch Size: 111 × 74 yards	**Web Site**: www.liverpoolfc.tv

GENERAL INFORMATION

Car Parking: None available in the immediate area
Coach Parking: Priory Road and Pinehurst Avenue
Nearest Railway Station: Kirkdale (¾ mile)
Nearest Bus Station: Paradise Street, Liverpool
Club Shop: At the ground, at Williamson Square and
'Liverpool One' in the City Centre and in Chester City Centre
Opening Times: At Anfield: Monday to Friday 9.00am to
5.00pm, Saturdays 9.30am to 4.00pm; At Williamson Square
and Chester: Monday to Friday 9.00am to 5.30pm;
At Liverpool One: Monday to Friday 9.30am to 8.00pm,
Saturdays 9.00am – 7.00pm and Sundays 11.00am – 5.00pm
Telephone Nº: (0151) 263-2361

GROUND INFORMATION

Away Supporters' Entrances & Sections:
Anfield Road

ADMISSION INFO (2012/2013 PRICES)

Adult Seating: £42.00 – £48.00
Adult Kop Seating: £39.00 – £45.00
Senior Citizen Seating: £31.50 – £36.00
Senior Citizen Kop Seating: £29.50 – £34.00
Child Seating: £15.00 – accompanied by a paying adult
Note: Prices vary depending on the category of the game
Programme Price: £3.00

DISABLED INFORMATION

Wheelchairs: 100 spaces are available in total in the
Paddock Enclosure, Kop Stand and Anfield Road Stand.
8 of these spaces are reserved for away fans.
Helpers: One helper is admitted per wheelchair but a
second helper can sometimes be accommodated
Prices: £29.50 – £36.00 for the disabled. One helper is
admitted free of charge with each disabled fan.
Disabled Toilets: Two available in the Paddock, two in the
Kop Stand and one in the Anfield Road Stand
Commentaries are available for the visually impaired on request
Contact: (0151) 423-5676 Disability Liaison Officer
(Bookings are necessary)   **E-mail**: disability@liverpoolfc.tv

Travelling Supporters' Information:
Routes: From the North: Exit the M6 at Junction 28 and follow Liverpool A580 signs into Walton Hall Avenue, pass Stanley
Park and turn left into Anfield Road; From the South and East: Take the M62 to the end of the motorway, then turn right into
Queen's Drive (A5058) and turn left after 3 miles into Utting Avenue. After 1 mile, turn right into Anfield Road; From North
Wales: Take the Mersey Tunnel into the City Centre and follow signs for Preston (A580) into Walton Hall Avenue. Turn right into
Anfield Road before Stanley Park.

MANCHESTER CITY FC

Founded: 1887 (**Entered League**: 1892)
Former Name: St.Mark's FC, Ardwick FC (1887-1894)
Nickname: 'Citizens' 'City' 'Blues'
Ground: Etihad Stadium, Etihad Campus, Manchester M11 3FF
Ground Capacity: 47,726 (All seats)
Record Attendance: 47,422 (vs Spurs – 2012)

Pitch Size: 115 × 75 yards
Colours: Sky Blue shirts with White shorts
Telephone Nº: (0161) 444-1894
Ticket Office: (0161) 444-1894
Fax Number: (0161) 438-7999
Web Site: www.mcfc.co.uk
E-mail: mcfc@mcfc.co.uk

GENERAL INFORMATION

Car Parking: 1,000 spaces available at the stadium. Another 7,000 spaces are available off site in the vicinity.
Coach Parking: Around 40 spaces available at the stadium
Nearest Railway Station: Ashburys (15 minutes walk) or Manchester Piccadilly (20 minutes walk)
Nearest Bus Station: 53, 54, 185, 186, 216, 217, 230, 231, 232, 233, 234, 235, 236, X36 and X37 services all stop at the stadium
Club Shop: At the stadium + Market Street, Manchester
Opening Times: Monday to Saturday 9.00am to 5.30pm, Sundays 11.00am to 5.00pm and before and after matches. Market Street: Monday to Saturday 9.00am to 8.00pm (until 7.00pm on Saturdays), Sundays 11.00am to 5.00pm
Telephone Nº: 0870 062-1894

GROUND INFORMATION

Away Supporters' Entrances & Sections: South Stand

ADMISSION INFO (2011/2012 PRICES)

Adult Seating: £20.00 – £52.00
Child Seating: £5.00 – £25.00
Senior Citizen Seating: £18.00 – £37.00
Note: Prices vary depending on the category of the game and the location of the seating
Programme Price: £3.00

DISABLED INFORMATION

Wheelchairs: 197 spaces available in total
Helpers: One helper admitted per wheelchair
Prices: £14.00 – £21.00 per disabled fan
Disabled Toilets: Available in all stands
Commentaries for the blind and lifts are also available
Contact: (0161) 438-7747 (Bookings are recommended)

Travelling Supporters' Information:
Routes: From the North: Exit the M60 at Junction 23 onto the A662 Ashton New Road. The stadium is approximately 1½ miles on the right hand side; From the East: Take the A635 which becomes the A662 Ashton New Road. Then as from the North; From the South: Take the M56 onto the M60. Join the A34 Kingsway at Junction 3. Follow the A34 until you join the A6010 Alan Turing Way. The Stadium is situated on the left, after approximately 2½ miles; From the West: Take the M61 to the M60. Exit at Junction 23, then follow directions as from the North.

MANCHESTER UNITED FC

Founded: 1878 (**Entered League**: 1892)
Former Names: Newton Heath LYR FC (1878-1892),
Newton Heath FC (1892-1902)
Nickname: 'Red Devils'
Ground: Sir Matt Busby Way, Old Trafford,
Manchester   M16 0RA
Ground Capacity: 76,022 (All seats)
Record Attendance: 76,962 (25th March 1939)

Pitch Size: 115 × 76 yards
Colours: Red shirts with White shorts
Telephone N°: (0161) 868-8000
Ticket Information: (0161) 868-8000
Fax Number: (0161) 868-8804
Web Site: www.manutd.com
E-mail: enquiries@manutd.co.uk

GENERAL INFORMATION

Car Parking: Lancashire Cricket Ground and Car Park E3 on John Gilbert Way. Other approved car parks are signposted
Coach Parking: By Police direction
Nearest Railway Station: At the ground
Nearest Bus Station: Chorlton Street
Nearest Metro Station: Old Trafford, located at L.C.C.C. and also Salford Quays
Club Shop: At the ground
Opening Times: Weekdays 9.00am – 5.30pm; Matchdays 9.00am to kick-off + 1 hour after match; Sundays 10.30am – 4.30pm; Non-match Saturdays 9.00am – 5.00pm
Telephone N°: (0161) 868-8000
Museum & Tour Centre: (0161) 868-8000

GROUND INFORMATION

Away Supporters' Entrances & Sections:
South Stand (turnstile 22) & East Stand (turnstile 30)

ADMISSION INFO (2012/2013 PRICES)

Adult Seating: £30.00 – £57.00
Senior Citizen/Ages 16 to 17 Seating: £16.00 – £27.00
Ages 18 to 20 Seating: £23.00 – £44.50
Under-16s Seating: £12.00 (Members only)
Note: Members of the club receive discounted prices
Programme Price: £3.00

DISABLED INFORMATION

Wheelchairs: 104 spaces in total for Home and Away fans in the disabled section – in front of 'L' Stand
Helpers: One helper admitted per disabled person
Prices: Free of charge for the disabled and helpers
Disabled Toilets: Located near the disabled section
Commentaries are available for the visually impaired
Contact: (0161) 868-8000   (Bookings are necessary)

Travelling Supporters' Information:
Routes: From the North and West: Take the M61 to the M60 and exit at Junction 4 following Manchester (A5081) signs. Turn right after 2½ miles into Sir Matt Busby Way for the ground; From the South: Exit the M6 at Junction 19 and take Stockport (A556) road then Altrincham (A56). From Altrincham follow Manchester signs and turn left into Sir Matt Busby Way after 6 miles; From the East: Exit the M62 at Junction 17 and take the A56 to Manchester. Follow signs for the South then signs for Chester (Chester Road). Turn right into Sir Matt Busby Way after 2 miles.

MIDDLESBROUGH FC

Founded: 1876 (**Entered League**: 1899)	**Colours**: Shirts and shorts are Red with White trim
Nickname: 'Boro'	**Telephone Nº**: 0844 499-6789
Ground: Riverside Stadium, Middlesbrough, TS3 6RS	**Ticket Office**: 0844 499-1234
Ground Capacity: 34,998 (All seats)	**Fax Number**: (01642) 757697
Record Attendance: 34,836 (28th December 2004)	**Web Site**: www.mfc.co.uk
Pitch Size: 115 × 75 yards	**E-mail**: enquiries@mfc.co.uk

GENERAL INFORMATION

Car Parking: 1,250 spaces available
Coach Parking: At the ground
Nearest Railway Station: Middlesbrough (½ mile)
Nearest Bus Station: Middlesbrough
Club Shops: At ground and Captain Cook Square
Opening Times: Weekdays 9.30am – 5.00pm and Saturday Matchdays 9.30am until kick-off; Captain Cook Square: Monday to Saturday 9.00am – 5.30pm
Telephone Nº: 0844 499-2676

GROUND INFORMATION

Away Supporters' Entrances & Sections:
South Stand turnstiles for the South Stand

ADMISSION INFO (2011/2012 PRICES)

Adult Seating: £24.00 – £31.00
Senior Citizen Seating: £17.00 – £23.00
Under-18s Seating: £14.00
Note: Prices vary depending on the area of the ground
Programme Price: £3.00

DISABLED INFORMATION

Wheelchairs: 170 spaces in total for home and away fans in the disabled areas in the West and South Stands
Helpers: One helper admitted per disabled person
Prices: £26.00 in total for each disabled fan and helper
Disabled Toilets: Available in the West and South Stands
Contact: 0844 499-1234 (Bookings are necessary)
E-mail contact: disability@mfc.co.uk

Travelling Supporters' Information:
Routes: From the North: Take the A19 across the flyover and join the A66 (Eastbound). At the end of the flyover, turn left at North Ormesby where the ground is well-signposted. The ground is 200 metres down the road; From the South: Take the A1 and A19 to the junction with the A66 (Eastbound). After the flyover, turn left at North Ormesby following signs for the ground.

MILLWALL FC

Founded: 1885 (**Entered League**: 1920)
Former Names: Millwall Rovers FC (1885-1893);
Millwall Athletic FC (1893-1925)
Nickname: 'Lions'
Ground: The Den, Zampa Road, London SE16 3LN
Ground Capacity: 20,146 (All seats)
Record Attendance: 20,093 (10th January 1994)

Pitch Size: 115 × 74 yards
Colours: Dark Blue shirts with White shorts
Telephone Nº: (020) 7232-1222
Ticket Office: (020) 7231-9999
Fax Number: (020) 7231-3663
Web Site: www.millwallfc.co.uk
E-mail: questions@millwallplc.com

GENERAL INFORMATION
Car Parking: Street parking
Coach Parking: Adjacent to the ground
Nearest Railway Station: New Cross Gate (1 mile) or
South Bermondsey (½ mile)
Nearest Tube: New Cross Gate (1 mile)/Canada Water (1 mile)
Club Shop: Next to the Stadium
Opening Times: Daily 9.30am to 4.30pm
Telephone Nº: (020) 7231-9845

GROUND INFORMATION
Away Supporters' Entrances & Sections:
North Stand turnstiles 31-36. A walkway from South
Bermondsey Station to the ground is open on matchdays

ADMISSION INFO (2012/2013 PRICES)
Adult Seating: £25.00 – £30.00
Under-16s Seating: £11.00 – £13.00
Under-12s Seating: £6.00 – £7.00
Concessionary Seating: £17.00 – £20.00
Note: Discounts are available for members' advance purchases
Programme Price: £3.00

DISABLED INFORMATION
Wheelchairs: 78 spaces in the disabled section in the West
Stand and 17 spaces for away fans in front of the North Stand
Helpers: One helper admitted per wheelchair disabled
Prices: Standard prices for the disabled. Free for helpers
Disabled Toilets: 17 toilets available around the Stadium
Commentaries are available for the blind
Contact: (020) 7232-1222   (Bookings are necessary)

Travelling Supporters' Information:
Routes: From the North: Follow City signs from the M1/A1 then signs for Shoreditch & Whitechapel. Follow Ring Road signs for Dover, cross over Tower Bridge and after 1 mile take 1st exit at the roundabout onto the A2. From Elephant and Castle take the A2 (New Kent Road) into Old Kent Road and turn left after 4 miles into Ilderton Road to Zampa Road; From the South: Take the A20 & A21 following signs to London. At New Cross follow signs for Surrey Quays into Kender Street, turn left into Old Kent Road then right into Ilderton Road. Zampa Road is the 7th turning on the right; From the East: Take the A2 to New Cross (then as from the South); From the West: From M4 & M3 follow the South Circular (A205) then follow signs for Clapham, the City (A3) then Camberwell to New Cross and then as from South.

MILTON KEYNES DONS FC

Founded: 2005
Former Names: None
Nickname: 'Dons'
Ground: *stadium*mk, Stadium Way West, Milton Keynes   MK1 1ST
Ground Capacity: 22,000 at present (All seats)
Pitch Size: 110 × 74 yards

Colours: White with Black and Gold trim
Telephone Nº: (01908) 622922
Ticket Office: (01908) 622900
Fax Number: (01908) 622933
Web Site: www.mkdons.com
E-mail: info@mkdons.com

GENERAL INFORMATION
Car Parking: 2,000 Pay and Display spaces at the Stadium
Coach Parking: By Police direction
Nearest Railway Station: Bletchley (1 mile)
Nearest Bus Station: Bletchley
Club Shop: At the Stadium
Opening Times: Weekdays 9.00am to 5.00pm with extended hours on Matchdays
Telephone Nº: (01908) 622922

GROUND INFORMATION
Away Supporters' Entrances & Sections:
North Stand corner, Gate 3

ADMISSION INFO (2012/2013 PRICES)
Adult Seating: £20.00
Concessionary Seating: £15.00
Under-18s Seating: £5.00
Note: Under-7s are admitted free of charge if they are members of the club
Programme Price: £2.50

DISABLED INFORMATION
Wheelchairs: Accommodated around the ground at concourse level
Helpers: One helper admitted per disabled person
Prices: Concessionary prices for the disabled. Helpers are admitted free of charge
Disabled Toilets: Available
Contact: (01908) 622900   (Bookings are necessary)

Travelling Supporters' Information:
Routes: From all parts: Exit the M1 at Junction 14, following signs for Milton Keynes and cross the first roundabout onto H6 Childs Way. Turn left at the next roundabout onto V11 Tongwell Street. Continue along this road then turn right at the third roundabout onto H9 Groveway. Continue along Groveway then take the first exit at the fourth roundabout towards Central Bletchley. Stadium:MK is the first turning on the left.

MORECAMBE FC

Founded: 1920   (**Entered League**: 2007)
Former Names: None
Nickname: 'Shrimps'
Ground: Globe Arena, Christie Way, Westgate, Morecambe LA4 4TB
Record Attendance: 9,324 (1962 – Christie Park)
Pitch Size: 110 × 73 yards

Colours: Red shirts with White shorts
Telephone Nº: (01524) 411797
Daytime Phone Nº: (01524) 411797
Fax Number: (01524) 832230
Ground Capacity: 6,354
Seating Capacity: 2,200
Web site: www.morecambefc.com
E-mail: office@morecambefc.com

GENERAL INFORMATION

Car Parking: Available at a school adjacent to the ground
Coach Parking: Available at the rear of the stadium
Nearest Railway Station: Morecambe Central (2 miles)
Nearest Bus Station: Morecambe
Club Shop: At the ground
Opening Times: Weekdays & Matchdays 9.00am to 5.00pm
Telephone Nº: (01524) 411797

GROUND INFORMATION

Away Supporters' Entrances & Sections:
Bay Radio (East) Away Stand plus seating in part of the Main Stand.

ADMISSION INFO (2012/2013 PRICES)

Adult Standing: £14.00 – £15.00
Adult Seating: £19.00 – £24.00
Ages 12 to 18 Standing: £5.00 (Under-11s free of charge)
Ages 12 to 18 Seating: £6.00 – £24.00
Ages 5 to 11 Seating: From free to £24.00
Senior Citizen Standing: £11.00 – £12.00
Senior Citizen Seating: £15.00 – £23.00
Note: Family Tickets are available and other discounts for children are also available in the Family Enclosure
Programme Price: £3.00

DISABLED INFORMATION

Wheelchairs: Accommodated
Prices: Concessionary prices are charged
Disabled Toilets: Available in all stands
Contact: (01524) 411797   (Bookings are preferred)

Travelling Supporters' Information:
Routes: Exit the M6 at Junction 34 and follow signs to Morecambe. Cross the River Lune via the Greyhound Bridge and continue, following signs for Morecambe onto the A589. At the first two roundabouts, keep in the right hand lane and carry straight on. Turn left at the third roundabout (Shrimp) and continue along Westgate for about a mile. Globe Stadium is on the right.
Away fans car parking: Turn right after the Junior School towards Venture Caravan Park and the away car park is signposted.

NEWCASTLE UNITED FC

Founded: 1882 (**Entered League**: 1893)
Former Names: Newcastle East End FC (1882-1892) amalgamated with Newcastle West End FC
Nickname: 'Magpies'
Ground: SportsDirect Arena, Newcastle-Upon-Tyne, NE1 4ST
Ground Capacity: 52,420 (All seats)

Record Attendance: 68,386 (3rd September 1930)
Pitch Size: 115 × 74 yards
Colours: Black and White striped shirts, Black shorts
Telephone Nº: 0844 372-1892
Ticket Office: 0844 372-1892
Web Site: www.nufc.co.uk
E-mail: boxoffice@nufc.co.uk

GENERAL INFORMATION

Car Parking: Street parking
Coach Parking: By Police direction
Nearest Railway Station: Newcastle Central (¼ mile)
Nearest Bus Station: St. James' Boulevard (¼ mile)
Club Shop: At the ground, Eldon Way and the MetroCentre
Opening Times: All shops are open Monday to Saturday 9.00am – 5.00pm; Eldon open until 8.00pm on Thursdays; MetroCentre open until at least 7.00pm Monday to Saturday
Telephone Nº: 0844 372-1892

GROUND INFORMATION

Away Supporters' Entrances & Sections:
Rear of the Sir John Hall Stand, entrance from Barrack Road

ADMISSION INFO (2011/2012 PRICES)

Adult Seating: £20.00 – £45.00
Child Seating: £10.00 – £23.00 (in the Family Seating Area)
Senior Citizen Seating: £15.00 – £34.00
Programme Price: £3.00

DISABLED INFORMATION

Wheelchairs: 103 spaces in total in the disabled areas throughout the stadium
Helpers: One helper admitted per disabled person
Prices: Prices available on application
Disabled Toilets: Available throughout the stadium
Commentaries are available for 20 blind supporters
Contact: Please contact the Ticket Office for information

Travelling Supporters' Information:
Routes: From the North: Follow the A1 into Newcastle, then follow Hexham signs into Percy Street. Turn right into Leazes Park Road; From the South: Take the A1M, then after Birtley Granada Services take the A1 Gateshead Western Bypass (bear left on the Motorway). Follow Airport signs for approximately 3 miles then take the A692 (Newcastle) sign, crossing the Redheugh Bridge. Proceed over three sets of traffic lights to the roundabout and take the 1st exit into Barrack Road; From the West: Take the A69 towards the City Centre. Pass Newcastle General Hospital. At the traffic lights after the Hospital turn left into Brighton Grove. After 70 yards turn right into Stanhope Street and proceed into Barrack Road for the ground.

NORTHAMPTON TOWN FC

Founded: 1897 (**Entered League**: 1920)
Nickname: 'Cobblers'
Ground: Sixfields Stadium, Upton Way,
Northampton NN5 5QA
Ground Capacity: 7,653 (All seats)
Record Attendance: 7,557 (26th September 1998)
Pitch Size: 116 × 72 yards

Colours: Claret and White shirts with White shorts
Telephone Nº: (01604) 757773
Ticket Office: (01604) 588338
Fax Number: (01604) 751613
Web Site: www.ntfc.co.uk

GENERAL INFORMATION

Car Parking: At the ground
Coach Parking: At the ground
Nearest Railway Station: Northampton Castle (2 miles)
Nearest Bus Station: Greyfriars
Club Shop: At the ground
Opening Times: Monday to Thursday 10.00am – 5.00pm,
Friday 10.00am – 7.00pm, non-match Saturdays 10.00am –
12.00pm and Matchdays 10.00am to kick-off and 30 minutes
after the final whistle
Telephone Nº: (01604) 757773

GROUND INFORMATION

Away Supporters' Entrances & Sections:
Paul Cox Panel & Paint Stand

ADMISSION INFO (2012/2013 PRICES)

Adult Seating: £19.00 – £20.00
Senior Citizen Seating: £14.00 – £16.00
Under-21s Seating: £14.00 – £16.00 (Members only)
Under-18s Seating: £7.00 – £8.00
Under-7s: Admitted free of charge
Note: A range of concessionary prices are available
Programme Price: £2.00

DISABLED INFORMATION

Wheelchairs: 80 spaces in total for Home and Away fans in
various areas of the ground
Helpers: One helper admitted per disabled person
Prices: £14.00 for disabled fans. Free of charge for helpers
Disabled Toilets: Available by the disabled areas
Commentaries are available for the blind
Contact: (01604) 588338 (Bookings are necessary)

Travelling Supporters' Information:
Routes: From All Parts: Exit the M1 at Junction 15A following the signs for Sixfields Leisure onto Upton Way – the ground is
approximately 2 miles.

NORWICH CITY FC

Founded: 1902 (**Entered League**: 1920)
Nickname: 'Canaries'
Ground: Carrow Road, Norwich NR1 1JE
Ground Capacity: 27,000 (All seats)
Record Attendance: 43,984 (30th March 1963)
Pitch Size: 114 × 74 yards

Colours: Yellow shirts with Green shorts
Telephone Nº: (01603) 760760
Ticket Office: 0844 826-1902
Fax Number: (01603) 613886
Web Site: www.canaries.co.uk
E-mail: reception@ncfc-canaries.co.uk

GENERAL INFORMATION

Car Parking: City Centre car parks (nearby)
Coach Parking: Lower Clarence Road
Nearest Railway Station: Norwich Thorpe (1 mile)
Nearest Bus Station: Surrey Street, Norwich
Club Shop: Temporary shop in the Jarrold Stand
Opening Times: Weekdays & Matchdays 9.00am to 5.00pm
Telephone Nº: (01603) 760760

GROUND INFORMATION

Away Supporters' Entrances & Sections:
Jarrold Stand usings turnstiles 51-57

ADMISSION INFO (2012/2013 PRICES)

Please contact the club for details of ticket prices and availability for the 2012/2013 season.

DISABLED INFORMATION

Wheelchairs: 74 spaces for home fans and 15 for away fans in Jarrold/Aviva Community Stand. Plenty of spaces are also available for ambulant disabled fans
Helpers: One helper admitted per disabled person
Prices: A single price is charged for each disabled fan and helper
Disabled Toilets: Available within the disabled area
Contact: 0844 826-1902   (Bookings are necessary)

Travelling Supporters' Information:
Routes: From the South: Take the A11 or A140 and turn right onto the A47 towards Great Yarmouth & Lowestoft, take the A146 Norwich/Lowestoft sliproad, turn left towards Norwich and follow road signs for the Football Ground; From the West: Take the A47 on to the A146 Norwich/Lowestoft slip road. Turn left towards Norwich, follow the road signs for the Football Ground.

NOTTINGHAM FOREST FC

Founded: 1865 (**Entered League**: 1892)
Nickname: 'The Reds'
Ground: The City Ground, Nottingham   NG2 5FJ
Ground Capacity: 30,602 (All seats)
Record Attendance: 49,946 (28th October 1967)
Pitch Size: 112 × 76 yards

Colours: Red shirts with White shorts
Telephone Nº: (0115) 982-4444
Ticket Office: 0871 226-1980
Fax Number: (0115) 982-4455
Web Site: www.nottinghamforest.co.uk
E-mail: feedback@nottinghamforest.co.uk

GENERAL INFORMATION

Car Parking: East car park (limited) and street parking
Coach Parking: East car park, Meadow Lane
Nearest Railway Station: Nottingham Midland (½ mile)
Nearest Bus Station: Victoria Street/Broadmarsh Centre
Club Shop: At the ground
Opening Times: Weekdays 9.00am – 5.00pm; Matchdays 9.00am – kick-off and 30 minutes after the game; Sunday matchdays 10.00am – kick-off + 30 minutes after the game
Telephone Nº: (0115) 982-4499

GROUND INFORMATION

Away Supporters' Entrances & Sections:
Entrances via East car park for Bridgford Stand

ADMISSION INFO (2011/2012 PRICES)

Adult Seating: £20.00 – £37.00
Under-18s: £12.00
Under-12s: £6.00
Concessionary Seating: £15.00 – £22.00
Note: Discounts are available for tickets purchased in advance
Programme Price: £3.00

DISABLED INFORMATION

Wheelchairs: 12 spaces in the Brian Clough Stand, up to 22 spaces in the Lower Bridgford Stand, 12 spaces in the Upper Bridgford Stand and 13 spaces in Trent End "Castle Suite".
Helpers: One helper admitted per disabled person
Prices: Prices vary depending on the fixture. Please contact the club for further information
Disabled Toilets: Available in the Executive Stand
Contact: (0115) 982-4341   (Bookings are necessary)

Travelling Supporters' Information:
Routes: From the North: Exit the M1 at Junction 26 following Nottingham signs (A610) then signs to Melton Mowbray and Trent Bridge (A606). Cross the River Trent, turn left into Radcliffe Road then left again into Colwick Road for the ground; From the South: Exit the M1 at Junction 24 following signs for Nottingham (South) to Trent Bridge. Turn right into Radcliffe Road then left into Colwick Road; From the East: Take the A52 to West Bridgford and follow signs for Football & Cricket; From the West: Take the A52 into Nottingham, follow signs for Melton Mowbray and Trent Bridge, cross the River Trent (then as North).

NOTTS COUNTY FC

Founded: 1862 (**Entered League**: 1888)
Nickname: 'The Magpies'
Ground: Meadow Lane, Nottingham   NG2 3HJ
Ground Capacity: 20,300 (All seats)
Record Attendance: 47,310 (12th March 1955)
Pitch Size: 113 × 70 yards

Colours: Black and White striped shirts, Black shorts
Telephone Nº: (0115) 952-9000
Ticket Office: (0115) 952-9000
Fax Number: (0115) 955-3994
Web Site: www.nottscountyfc.co.uk
E-mail: office@nottscountyfc.co.uk

GENERAL INFORMATION

Car Parking: British Waterways, Meadow Lane
Coach Parking: Incinerator Road (Cattle Market Corner)
Nearest Railway Station: Nottingham Midland (½ mile)
Nearest Bus Station: Broadmarsh Centre
Club Shop: At the ground
Opening Times: Mondays to Friday 9.00am – 5.00pm,
Saturday Matchdays 9.00am – 5.30pm, other Saturdays
9.00am – 1.00pm
Telephone Nº: (0115) 955-7200

GROUND INFORMATION

Away Supporters' Entrances & Sections:
Jimmy Sirrel Stand, Block Z – use Turnstiles 19-24

ADMISSION INFO (2012/2013 PRICES)

Adult Seating: £22.00 – £24.00
Under-16s Seating: £6.00
Concessionary Seating: £15.00
Programme Price: £3.00

DISABLED INFORMATION

Wheelchairs: 70 spaces in total in the disabled area,
County Road/Meadow Lane End corner
Helpers: One helper admitted per disabled fan
Prices: 25% reduction from normal prices for the disabled.
Helpers are admitted free of charge
Disabled Toilets: Available next to the disabled area
Contact: (0115) 955-7204 (Bookings are necessary)

Travelling Supporters' Information:
Routes: From the North: Exit the M1 at Junction 26 following Nottingham signs (A610) then Melton Mowbray and Trent
Bridge (A606) signs. Before the River Trent turn left into Meadow Lane; From the South: Exit the M1 at Junction 24 following
signs for Nottingham (South) to Trent Bridge, cross the river and follow the one-way system to the right, then turn left and right
at the traffic lights then second right into Meadow Lane; From the East: Take the A52 to West Bridgford/Trent Bridge, cross the
river and follow the one-way system to the right then turn left and right at the traffic lights, then second right into Meadow
Lane; From the West: Take the A52 into Nottingham following signs for Melton Mowbray and Trent Bridge. Before the River
Trent turn left into Meadow Lane.

OLDHAM ATHLETIC FC

Founded: 1895 (**Entered League**: 1907)
Former Names: Pine Villa FC (1895-1899)
Nickname: 'Latics'
Ground: Boundary Park, Oldham   OL1 2PA
Ground Capacity: 10,904 (All seats)
Record Attendance: 47,671 (25th January 1930)
Pitch Size: 110 × 72 yards

Colours: Royal Blue shirts with White shorts and socks
Telephone Nº: (0161) 624-4972
Ticket Office: (0161) 785-5150
Fax Number: (0161) 627-5915
Web Site: www.oldhamathletic.co.uk
E-mail: enquiries@oldhamathletic.co.uk

GENERAL INFORMATION

Car Parking: Broadway Stand car park (1,000 cars)
Coach Parking: At the ground
Nearest Railway Station: Oldham Werneth (1½ miles)
Nearest Bus Station: Oldham Town Centre (2 miles)
Club Shop: At the ground
Opening Times: Mondays to Fridays 9.00am to 5.00pm.
Saturdays 9.00am to 12.00pm
Telephone Nº: (0161) 785-5169

GROUND INFORMATION

Away Supporters' Entrances & Sections:
Rochdale Road Stand

ADMISSION INFO (2012/2013 PRICES)

Adult Seating: £19.00 – £20.00
Senior Citizen Seating: £9.00 – £10.00
Junior Seating: £5.00 – £10.00
Programme Price: £3.00

DISABLED INFORMATION

Wheelchairs: 60 spaces in the disabled areas –
Broadway Paddock, Chadderton Road Stand and Rochdale
Road Stand
Helpers: One helper admitted per disabled person
Prices: Normal prices for the disabled. Free for helpers
Disabled Toilets: Available in Broadway Paddock and the
Rochdale Road Stand
Contact: (0161) 785-5179   (Bookings are necessary)

Travelling Supporters' Information:
Routes: From All Parts: Exit the M62 at Junction 20 and take the A627M to the junction with the A664. Take the 1st exit at the
roundabout onto Broadway, then the 1st right into Hilbre Avenue which leads to the car park at the ground.

OXFORD UNITED FC

Founded: 1893 (**Re-Entered League**: 2010)
Former Names: Headington United FC (1893-1960)
Nickname: 'U's'
Ground: Kassam Stadium, Grenoble Road, Oxford, OX4 4XP
Ground Capacity: 12,500 (All seats)
Record Attendance: 22,730 (At the Manor Ground)

Pitch Size: 115 × 71 yards
Colours: Yellow shirts with Navy Blue shorts
Telephone Nº: (01865) 337500
Ticket Office: (01865) 337533
Fax Number: (01865) 337501
Web Site: www.oufc.co.uk
E-mail: admin@oufc.co.uk

GENERAL INFORMATION

Car Parking: 2,000 free spaces available at the ground
Coach Parking: At the ground
Nearest Railway Station: Oxford (4 miles)
Nearest Bus Station: Oxford
Club Shop: At the ground
Opening Times: Monday to Friday 10.00am – 5.00pm and Matchdays from 10.00am until kick-off
Telephone Nº: (01865) 335310

GROUND INFORMATION

Away Supporters' Entrances & Sections:
North Stand turnstiles for North Stand accommodation. Ticket office for away supporters is adjacent

ADMISSION INFO (2012/2013 PRICES)

Adult Seating: £17.00 – £23.00
Under-16s Seating: £4.00 – £14.50 (Under-7s free)
Student Seating: £14.00 – £18.00
Senior Citizen Seating: £9.00 – £14.50
Note: Tickets are cheaper if bought prior to the matchday
Programme Price: £3.00

DISABLED INFORMATION

Wheelchairs: Accommodated in areas in the North, East and South Stands
Helpers: One assistant admitted per disabled person
Prices: Normal prices for the disabled. One assistant admitted free of charge per disabled fan if required
Disabled Toilets: Available throughout the ground
Commentaries are available for the visually impaired
Contact: (01865) 337533 (Bookings are not necessary)

Travelling Supporters' Information:
Routes: From the Oxford Ring Road take the A423 towards Henley and Reading then turn left after ½ mile following signs for the Oxford Science Park. Bear left and go straight on at two roundabouts then the Stadium is on the left in Grenoble Road. The Kassam Stadium is clearly signposted on all major roads in Oxford.

PETERBOROUGH UNITED FC

Founded: 1934 (**Entered League**: 1960)
Nickname: 'Posh'
Ground: London Road, Peterborough   PE2 8AL
Ground Capacity: 14,793
Seating Capacity: 8,631
Record Attendance: 30,096 (20th February 1965)
Pitch Size: 112 × 71 yards

Colours: Cobalt Blue shirts with White shorts
Telephone Nº: (01733) 865674
Ticket Office: 0844 847-1934
Fax Number: (01733) 344140
Web Site: www.theposh.com
E-mail: info@theposh.com

GENERAL INFORMATION

Car Parking: At the ground and also adjacent
Coach Parking: In front of the (North) Main Stand
Nearest Railway Station: Peterborough (1 mile)
Nearest Bus Station: Peterborough (1 mile)
Club Shop: At the ground
Opening Times: Monday to Thursday 9.00am to 5.00pm, Fridays 10.00am to 5.00pm and Saturday Matchdays 10.00pm to 3.00pm then 5.00pm to 5.30pm
Telephone Nº: (01733) 563947

GROUND INFORMATION

Away Supporters' Entrances & Sections:
A North Block (Seating) and Moyes End (Terrace)
(Note: Moyes End is being redeveloped during 2011/2012)

ADMISSION INFO (2012/2013 PRICES)

Adult Standing: £15.00 – £20.00
Adult Seating: £20.00 – £25.00
Senior Citizen Standing/Seating: £11.00 – £15.00
Student Standing/Seating: £11.00 – £15.00
Under-16s Standing/Seating: £8.00 – £12.00
Under-16s Seating: £5.00 in the Family Stand
Note: Under-10s are admitted free in the Family Stand but must be accompanied by a paying adult.
Prices vary depending on the category of the game
Programme Price: £3.00

DISABLED INFORMATION

Wheelchairs: 36 spaces available in total
Helpers: One helper admitted per disabled person
Prices: Normal prices for the disabled. Free for helpers
Disabled Toilets: Available in the South and Main Stands
Contact: (01733) 563947   (Bookings are necessary)

Travelling Supporters' Information:
Routes: From the North and West: Take the A1 then the A47 into the Town Centre and follow Whittlesey signs across the river into London Road; From the East: Take the A47 into the Town Centre (then as from the North); From the South: Take the A1 then the A15 into London Road.

PLYMOUTH ARGYLE FC

Founded: 1886 (**Entered League**: 1920)
Former Names: Argyle FC (1886-1903)
Nickname: 'Pilgrims' 'Argyle'
Ground: Home Park, Plymouth   PL2 3DQ
Ground Capacity: 19,500 (All seats)
Record Attendance: 43,596 (10th October 1936)
Pitch Size: 112 × 72 yards

Colours: Green shirts and White shorts
Telephone N°: (01752) 562561
Box Office: 0845 872-3335
Fax Number: (01752) 606167
Web Site: www.pafc.co.uk
E-mail: argyle@pafc.co.uk

GENERAL INFORMATION

Car Parking: Car park for 1,000 cars is adjacent
Coach Parking: Central Park Car Park
Nearest Railway Station: Plymouth North Road
Nearest Bus Station: Bretonside, Plymouth
Club Shop: At the ground and Drake Circus Shopping Mall
Opening Times: Ground shop: Monday to Friday 9.00am – 5.00pm, Non-match Saturdays 9.00am – 3.00pm, Saturday Matchdays 9.00am – 3.00pm + 30 minutes after the game. Drake Circus shop: Monday to Saturday 9.00am to 6.00pm (8.00pm on Thursdays). Also Sundays 10.30am – 4.30pm
Telephone N°: (01752) 562561

GROUND INFORMATION

Away Supporters' Entrances & Sections:
Barn Park End turnstiles for covered accommodation

ADMISSION INFO (2011/2012 PRICES)

Adult Seating: £20.00
Under-17s Seating: £7.00
Senior Citizen Seating: £15.00
Note: Family Tickets are also available
Programme Price: £3.00

DISABLED INFORMATION

Wheelchairs: 60 spaces Home fans and 25 spaces for Away fans in the disabled sections
Helpers: One helper admitted per disabled person
Prices: Normal prices for the disabled. Free for helpers
Disabled Toilets: Available throughout the stadium
Commentaries are available for the visually impaired
Contact: (01752) 562561   (Barry Hardman – Bookings are necessary)

Travelling Supporters' Information:
Routes: From All Parts: Take the A38 to Tavistock Road (A386), then branch left following signs for Home Park (A386) and continue for 1¼ miles. The car park for the ground is on the left (signposted Home Park).

PORTSMOUTH FC

Founded: 1898 (**Entered League**: 1920)
Nickname: 'Pompey'
Ground: Fratton Park, 57 Frogmore Road, Portsmouth, Hants   PO4 8RA
Ground Capacity: 21,178 (All seats)
Record Attendance: 51,385 (26th February 1949)
Pitch Size: 110 × 71 yards

Colours: Blue shirts and shorts
Telephone Nº: (023) 9273-1204
Ticket Office: 08442 777879
Fax Number: (023) 9273-4129
Web Site: www.portsmouthfc.co.uk
E-mail: info@pompeyfc.co.uk

GENERAL INFORMATION
Car Parking: Street parking
Coach Parking: By Police direction
Nearest Railway Station: Fratton (adjacent)
Nearest Bus Station: The Hard, Portsmouth
Club Shop: At the ground (Fratton Way)
Opening Times: Monday to Friday 9.30am – 5.30pm; Saturday matchdays 9.00am to 1 hour after the final whistle; Closed on Sundays
Telephone Nº: (023) 9273-8358

GROUND INFORMATION
Away Supporters' Entrances & Sections:
Aspley Road – Milton Road side for Aspley Road End

ADMISSION INFO (2012/2013 PRICES)
Adult Seating: £20.00   (£18.00 in the Family Section)
Junior Seating: £10.00   (£8.00 in the Family Section)
Senior Citizen Seating: £15.00 (£13.00 in Family Section)
Ages 17 to 22 Seating: £15.00 (£13.00 in Family Section)
Note: Adults/Senior Citizens or Ages 17 to 22 must be accompanied by a Junior to sit in the Family Section.
Programme Price: £3.00

DISABLED INFORMATION
Wheelchairs: Limited number of spaces available in the disabled section, Fratton End
Helpers: One helper admitted per disabled person
Prices: Not set at the time of going to press. Please contact the club for pricing information. Free of charge for helpers
Disabled Toilets: One available in disabled section
Contact: (023) 9273-1204   (Bookings are necessary)

Travelling Supporters' Information:
Routes: From the North and West: Take the M27 and M275 to the end then take the 2nd exit at the roundabout and after ¼ mile turn right at the 'T' junction into London Road (A2047). After 1¼ miles cross the railway bridge and turn left into Goldsmith Avenue. After ½ mile turn left into Frogmore Road; From the East: Take the A27 following Southsea signs (A2030). Turn left at the roundabout (3 miles) onto the A288, then right into Priory Crescent and next right into Carisbrooke Road for the ground.

PORT VALE FC

Founded: 1876 (**Entered League:** 1892)
Former Names: Burslem Port Vale FC
Nickname: 'Valiants'
Ground: Vale Park, Hamil Road, Burslem,
Stoke-on-Trent   ST6 1AW
Ground Capacity: 19,148 (All seats)
Record Attendance: 49,768 (20nd February 1960)
Pitch Size: 114 × 76 yards

Colours: White shirts Black & Gold trim, Black shorts
with Gold & White trim
Telephone Nº: (01782) 655800
Ticket Office: (01782) 655832
Fax Number: (01782) 834981
Web Site: www.port-vale.co.uk
E-mail: secretary@port-vale.co.uk

GENERAL INFORMATION
Car Parking: Car parks at the ground
Coach Parking: Hamil Road car park
Nearest Railway Station: Stoke
Nearest Bus Station: Burslem (adjacent)
Club Shop: At the ground
Opening Times: Monday to Saturday 9.00am – 5.00pm
Telephone Nº: (01782) 655833

GROUND INFORMATION
Away Supporters' Entrances & Sections:
Hamil Road turnstiles, numbers 1 to 8

ADMISSION INFO (2012/2013 PRICES)
Adult Seating: £21.50 – £22.50
Child Seating: £10.00   (Under-9s admitted free of charge)
Concessionary Seating: £16.00 – £16.50
Programme Price: £3.00

DISABLED INFORMATION
Wheelchairs: 46 spaces available in the Disabled Stand,
Lorne Street/Bycars Corner
Helpers: One helper admitted per disabled person
Prices: Normal prices for disabled fans. Free for helpers
Disabled Toilets: Available in the disabled area
Commentaries are available – please contact the club
Contact: (01782) 655832   (Bookings are necessary)

Travelling Supporters' Information:
Routes: From the North: Exit the M6 at Junction 16 and follow Stoke signs (A500). Branch left off the A500 at the exit signposted
Tunstall and take the 2nd exit at the roundabout into Newcastle Street. Proceed through the traffic lights into Moorland Road
and take the 2nd turning on the left into Hamil Road; From the South and West: Exit the M6 at Junction 15 and take the A5006
and A500. After 6¼ miles branch left (then as from the North); From the East: Take the A50 or A52 into Stoke following Burslem
signs into Waterloo Road, turn right at Burslem crossroads into Moorland Road (then as from the North).

PRESTON NORTH END FC

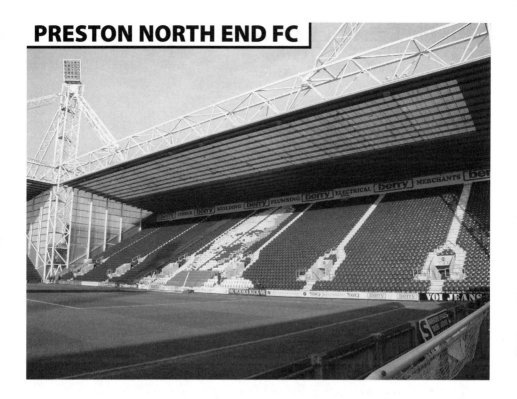

Founded: 1880 (**Entered League**: 1888)
Nickname: 'Lilywhites' 'North End'
Ground: Deepdale, Preston PR1 6RU
Ground Capacity: 23,404 (All seats)
Record Attendance: 42,684 (23rd April 1938)
Pitch Size: 109 × 77 yards (100 × 70 metres)

Colours: White shirts with Blue shorts
Telephone Nº: 0844 856-1964
Ticket Office: 0844 856-1966
Fax Number: (01772) 693366
Web Site: www.pne.com
E-mail: enquiries@pne.com

GENERAL INFORMATION

Car Parking: Four official car parks at the stadium plus further parking at Moor Park School
Coach Parking: By prior arrangement with the club
Nearest Railway Station: Preston (2 miles)
Nearest Bus Station: Preston (1 mile)
Club Shop: At the ground
Opening Times: Monday to Saturday 9.00am to 5.00pm and midweek matchdays 9.00am until kick-off
Telephone Nº: 0844 856-1965

GROUND INFORMATION

Away Supporters' Entrances & Sections:
Bill Shankly Kop

ADMISSION INFO (2012/2013 PRICES)

Adult Seating: £20.00 – £24.00
Under-16s Seating: £8.00 (Under-8s admitted free)
Ages 16 to 18/Student Seating: £14.00 – £18.00
Senior Citizen Seating: £14.00 – £18.00
Family Tickets: From £12.00 to £43.00
Programme Price: £3.00

DISABLED INFORMATION

Wheelchairs: Spaces available for advance order
Helpers: One helper admitted per wheelchair
Prices: £20.00 – £22.00 for the disabled. Free for helpers
Disabled Toilets: Available throughout the ground
Commentaries are available for the blind
Contact: 0844 856-1964 (Bookings are usually necessary)

Travelling Supporters' Information:
Routes: From the North: Take the M6 then the M55 to Junction 1. Follow signs for Preston (A6). After 2 miles turn left at the crossroads into Blackpool Road (A5085). Turn right ¾ mile into Deepdale; From the South and East: Exit the M6 at Junction 31 and follow Preston signs (A59). Take the 2nd exit at the roundabout (1 mile) into Blackpool Road. Turn left after 1¼ miles into Deepdale; From the West: Exit the M55 at Junction 1 (then as from the North).

QUEEN'S PARK RANGERS FC

Founded: 1882 (**Entered League**: 1920)
Former Names: Formed by the amalgamation of St. Jude's FC and Christchurch Rangers FC
Nickname: 'Rangers' 'R's'
Ground: Loftus Road Stadium, South Africa Road, London W12 7PJ
Ground Capacity: 18,309 (All seats)
Record Attendance: 35,353 (27th April 1974)

Pitch Size: 112 × 72 yards
Colours: Blue and White hooped shirts, White shorts
Telephone Nº: (020) 8743-0262
Ticket Office: 08444 777007
Fax Number: (020) 8749-0994
Web Site: www.qpr.co.uk

GENERAL INFORMATION
Car Parking: Street parking
Coach Parking: By Police direction
Nearest Railway Station: Ealing Broadway
Nearest Tube Station: White City (Central)
Club Shop: At the ground
Opening Times: Monday to Saturday 9.00am – 5.00pm and Sundays 10.00am – 4.00pm
Telephone Nº: (020) 8749-6862

GROUND INFORMATION
Away Supporters' Entrances & Sections:
South Africa Road turnstiles 13-15 & Ellerslie Road turnstiles 9-12 for School End Stand

ADMISSION INFO (2012/2013 PRICES)
Matchday admission prices for the 2012/2013 season were not set at the time we went to press so please contact the club for further pricing information.
Programme Price: £3.00

DISABLED INFORMATION
Wheelchairs: 25 spaces available in the disabled section
Helpers: One helper admitted per wheelchair
Prices: Concessionary prices for disabled. Free for helpers
Disabled Toilets: Available
Commentaries for the blind are available in the Ellerslie Road Stand
Contact: (020) 8740-2504   (Bookings are necessary)

Travelling Supporters' Information:
Routes: From the North: Take M1 & M406 North Circular for Neasden, go left after ¾ mile (A404) following signs for Harlesden, Hammersmith, past White City Stadium, right into White City Road and left into South Africa Road; From the South: Take A206 then A3 across Putney Bridge and follow signs to Hammersmith then Oxford (A219) to Shepherd's Bush. Join the A4020 following signs to Acton, turn right (¼ mile) into Loftus Road; From the East: Take the A12, A406 then the A503 to join the Ring Road, follow Oxford signs and join the A40(M), branch left (2 miles) to the M41, take the 3rd exit at the roundabout to the A4020 (then as South); From the West: Take the M4 to Chiswick then the A315 & A402 to Shepherd's Bush, join A4020 (then as South).

READING FC

Founded: 1871 (**Entered League**: 1920)
Former Names: Formed by the amalgamation of Hornets FC (1877) and Earley FC (1889)
Nickname: 'Royals'
Ground: Madejski Stadium, Junction 11 M4, Reading, Berkshire   RG2 0FL
Ground Capacity: 24,200 (All seats)
Record Attendance: 24,107 (3rd December 2004)

Pitch Size: 111 × 74 yards
Colours: Blue and White hooped shirts, White shorts
Telephone Nº: (0118) 968-1100
Ticket Office: 0844 249-1871
Fax Number: (0118) 968-1101
Web Site: www.readingfc.co.uk
E-mail: customerservice@readingfc.co.uk

GENERAL INFORMATION

Car Parking: 1,800 spaces available at the ground. Also another 2,000 spaces available nearby
Coach Parking: By Police direction (at the ground)
Nearest Railway Station: Reading Central
Nearest Bus Station: Reading
Club Shop: At the ground
Opening Times: Monday to Saturday 9.00am – 5.30pm, Sundays 10.00am – 4.00pm
Telephone Nº: (0118) 968-1234

GROUND INFORMATION

Away Supporters' Entrances & Sections:
South Stand entrances and accommodation

ADMISSION INFO (2012/2013 PRICES)

Adult Seating: £32.00 – £45.00
Concessionary Seating: £23.00 – £35.00
Under-16s Seating: £15.00 – £25.00
Note: Prices vary depending on the category of the game. Prices shown above are for tickets purchased in advance.
Programme Price: £3.00

DISABLED INFORMATION

Wheelchairs: A total of 128 spaces available for wheelchairs throughout the stadium
Helpers: Yes
Prices: £23.00–£26.00 for each disabled fan and one helper.
Disabled Toilets: One available adjacent to stand
Commentaries for approximately 12 people are available
Contact: (0118) 968-1006 (Bookings are necessary)

Travelling Supporters' Information:
Routes: The stadium is situated just off Junction 11 of the M4 near Reading.

ROCHDALE FC

Founded: 1907 (**Entered League**: 1921)
Former Names: Rochdale Town FC
Nickname: 'The Dale'
Ground: Spotland Stadium, Rochdale   OL11 5DS
Ground Capacity: 10,034
Seating Capacity: 7,913
Record Attendance: 24,231 (10th December 1949)

Pitch Size: 114 × 76 yards
Colours: Black and Blue striped shirts, White shorts
Telephone Nº: (01706) 644648
Ticket Office: (01706) 644648
Fax Number: (01706) 648466
Web Site: www.rochdaleafc.co.uk
E-mail: office@rochdaleafc.co.uk

GENERAL INFORMATION
Car Parking: Street parking only
Coach Parking: By Police direction
Nearest Railway Station: Rochdale (2 miles)
Nearest Bus Station: Town Centre (1 mile)
Club Shop: At the ground
Opening Times: Weekdays and Saturday Matchdays from 9.00am to 5.00pm
Telephone Nº: (01706) 644648

GROUND INFORMATION
Away Supporters' Entrances & Sections:
Turnstiles 11 to 18 for Willbutts Lane

ADMISSION INFO (2012/2013 PRICES)
Adult Standing: £15.00
Adult Seating: £18.00 – £20.00
Young Person/Senior Citizen Standing: £10.00
Young Person/Senior Citizen Seating: £12.00 – £14.00
Note: Under-8s are admitted free of charge and Family Tickets are also available
Programme Price: £3.00

DISABLED INFORMATION
Wheelchairs: 24 spaces in total in the disabled sections in the Main, Pearl Street and Willbutts Lane Stands
Helpers: One helper admitted per disabled person
Prices: Concessionary prices for disabled. Free for helpers
Disabled Toilets: Available adjacent to disabled area
Contact: (01706) 644648   (Bookings are necessary)

Travelling Supporters' Information:
Routes: From All Parts: Exit the M62 at Junction 20 and take the A627M signposted Rochdale. At the end of this link road, filter left carry on for 400 yards and go straight on at the roundabout into Roche Valley Way signposted Spotland Stadium. At the traffic lights go staight ahead and the ground is on the right after ½ mile.

ROTHERHAM UNITED FC

Founded: 1870 (**Entered League**: 1893)
Former Names: Rotherham Town FC (1870-1896), Thornhill United FC (1884-1905) and Rotherham County FC (1905-1925)
Nickname: 'The Millers'
Ground: New York Stadium, New York Way, Rotherham S60 1QY
Ground Capacity: 12,000 (All seats)
Pitch Size: 110 × 72 yards

Record Attendance: –
Colours: Red shirts with White sleeves, White shorts
Contact Telephone Nº: 08444 140733
Ticket Office: 08444 140737
Fax Number: 08444 140744
Web Site: www.themillers.co.uk
E-mail: office@rotherhamunited.net

GENERAL INFORMATION
Car Parking: At the ground and in Sheffield Road car park
Coach Parking: By police direction
Nearest Railway Station: Rotherham Central (½ mile)
Nearest Bus Station: Rotherham Town Centre (½ mile)
Club Shop: At the ground
Opening Times: Weekdays 9.00am to 5.00pm
Telephone Nº: 08444 140733

GROUND INFORMATION
Away Supporters' Entrances & Sections:
Morrison Stand

ADMISSION INFO (2012/2013 PRICES)
Adult Seating: £20.00 – £22.00
Senior Citizen/Student Seating: £12.00 – £14.00
Ages 8-15 Seating: £7.00 – £8.00
Note: Under-8s are admitted for free in the Family Stand
Programme Price: £2.50

DISABLED INFORMATION
Wheelchairs: Accommodated
Helpers: One helper admitted per disabled person
Prices: Disabled are charged concessionary prices. Helpers are admitted free of charge
Disabled Toilets: Available
Contact: 08444 140733 (Bookings are necessary)

Travelling Supporters' Information:
Routes: From the North: Exit the M1 at Junction 34, follow Rotherham (A6109) signs to the traffic lights and turn right. The ground is ¼ mile on the right; From the South & West: Exit the M1 at Junction 33, turn right and follow signs for Rotherham. Turn left at the roundabout then right at the next roundabout. Follow the dual carriageway and continue straight on at the next roundabout. Turn left at the following roundabout and the ground is on the left after ¼ mile; From the East: Take the A630 into Rotherham following Sheffield signs. Turn left at the 3rd roundabout (signposted Masborough) and the ground is on the right.

SCUNTHORPE UNITED FC

Founded: 1899 (**Entered League**: 1950)
Former Name: Scunthorpe and Lindsey United FC (1899-1912)
Nickname: 'The Iron'
Ground: Glanford Park, Doncaster Road, Scunthorpe, North Lincolnshire   DN15 8TD
Ground Capacity: 9,095
Seating Capacity: 6,322

Record Attendance: 8,906 (10th March 2007)
Pitch Size: 112 × 72 yards
Colours: Shirts and shorts are Claret with Sky Blue trim
Telephone Nº: 0871 221-1899
Ticket Office: 0871 221-1899
Fax Number: (01724) 857986
Web Site: www.scunthorpe-united.co.uk
E-mail: admin@scunthorpe-united.co.uk

GENERAL INFORMATION

Car Parking: Spaces for 800 cars at the ground
Coach Parking: At the ground
Nearest Railway Station: Scunthorpe (1½ miles)
Nearest Bus Station: Scunthorpe (1½ miles)
Club Shop: At the ground
Opening Times: Weekdays 9.00am to 5.00pm
Matchdays 10.00am to 3.00pm and 4.45pm to 5.15pm
Telephone Nº: (01724) 747682

GROUND INFORMATION

Away Supporters' Entrances & Sections:
Turnstiles 6-7 for the AMS Stand

ADMISSION INFO (2012/2013 PRICES)

Adult Standing: £17.00 – £18.00
Adult Seating: £21.00 – £30.00
Concessionary Standing: £12.00 – £13.00
Concessionary Seating: £14.00 – £23.00
Under-16s Standing: £5.00 – £6.00
Under-16s Seating: £5.00 – £6.00
Programme Price: £3.00

DISABLED INFORMATION

Wheelchairs: 10 spaces for Home fans and 6 spaces for Away fans in the disabled section, Grove Wharf Stand
Helpers: One helper admitted per disabled person
Prices: Normal prices for the disabled. Free for helpers
Disabled Toilets: One available in the disabled area
Commentaries are available for the blind
Contact: 0871-221-1899   (Bookings are necessary)

Travelling Supporters' Information:
Routes: From All Parts: Exit the M180 at Junction 3 onto the M181. Follow the M181 to the roundabout with the A18 and take the A18 towards Scunthorpe – the ground is on the right after 200 yards.

SHEFFIELD UNITED FC

Founded: 1889 (**Entered League**: 1892)
Nickname: 'Blades'
Ground: Bramall Lane, Sheffield   S2 4SU
Ground Capacity: 32,609 (All seats)
Record Attendance: 68,287 (15th February 1936)
Pitch Size: 110 × 73 yards

Colours: Red and White striped shirts, Black shorts
Telephone Nº: 0871 995-1899
Ticket Office: 0871 995-1889
Fax Number: 0871 663-2430
Web Site: www.sufc.co.uk
E-mail: info@sufc.co.uk

GENERAL INFORMATION

Car Parking: Street parking only
Coach Parking: By Police direction
Nearest Railway Station: Sheffield Midland (1 mile)
Nearest Bus Station: Pond Street, Sheffield (1 mile)
Club Shop: At the ground
Opening Times: Monday to Friday 9.30am – 5.30pm and
Matchdays from 9.00am – 5.30pm
Telephone Nº: 0871 663-2489

GROUND INFORMATION

Away Supporters' Entrances & Sections:
Visitors' Box Office – Bramall Lane Stand Lower Tier

ADMISSION INFO (2012/2013 PRICES)

Adult Seating: £18.00 – £26.00
Under-16s Seating: £9.50 – £14.00
Concessionary Seating: £14.00 – £19.00
Note: Prices vary depending on the category of the game
Programme Price: £4.00

DISABLED INFORMATION

Wheelchairs: Limited number of spaces available in the
disabled section – Members area
Helpers: One helper admitted per wheelchair
Prices: £10.00 for the disabled
Disabled Toilets: 7 available within the enclosure
Commentaries available for the blind on request
Contact: 0871 222-1889   (Bookings are necessary)

Travelling Supporters' Information:
Routes: From the North: Exit the M1 at Junction 33 following signs to Sheffield (A57) and continue along Sheffield Parkway until the Park Square roundabout. Take the 3rd exit and follow the A61 (Sheffield). Midland Station is on the left, the road veers to the left then take the middle lane following the ring road to the right. Take the first exit at the roundabout into Bramhall Lane.; From the South: Exit the M1 at junction 29 and take the A617 (Chesterfield). Take the 3rd exit at the roundabout onto the A61 and continue to the Earl of Arundel and Surrey Public House. Turn left and continue into Bramhall Lane; From the East: Exit the M1 at Junctions 31 or 33 and take the A57 to the roundabout, take the 3rd exit into Sheaf Street (then as from the North); From the West: Take the A57 into Sheffield and take the 4th exit at the roundabout into Upper Hanover Street and at the 2nd roundabout take the 3rd exit into Bramall Lane.

SHEFFIELD WEDNESDAY FC

Founded: 1867 (**Entered League**: 1892)
Former Name: The Wednesday FC
Nickname: 'Owls'
Ground: Hillsborough, Sheffield S6 1SW
Ground Capacity: 39,732 (All seats)
Record Attendance: 72,841 (17th February 1934)

Pitch Size: 116 × 75 yards
Colours: Blue and White striped shirts, Black shorts
Telephone Nº: 0871 995-1867
Ticket Hotline: 0871 900-1867
Web Site: www.swfc.co.uk
E-mail: enquiries@swfc.co.uk

GENERAL INFORMATION

Car Parking: Street parking
Coach Parking: Clay Wheels Lane
Nearest Railway Station: Sheffield Midland (4 miles)
Nearest Bus Station: Pond Street, Sheffield (4 miles)
Club Shop: At the ground
Ground Opening Times: Monday to Friday from 8.45am to 5.15pm and Saturday from 9.00am to 12.00pm
Telephone Nº: 0871 995-1867

GROUND INFORMATION

Away Supporters' Entrances & Sections:
West Stand turnstiles for West Stand, Upper Tier

ADMISSION INFO (2012/2013 PRICES)

Matchday admission prices had not been decided when we went to press so please contact the club directly for further pricing information.
Programme Price: £3.00

DISABLED INFORMATION

Wheelchairs: 88 spaces for home fans and 9 spaces for visiting fans in the disabled section of the North Stand & West Stand Lower. Ambulant disabled fans can sit in any section of the ground other than the Grandstand.
Helpers: Admitted
Prices: Normal prices for the disabled. Helpers free of charge
Disabled Toilets: Available in the North and West Stands
Commentaries are available for the blind
Contact: 0871 900-1867 (Bookings are necessary)

Travelling Supporters' Information:
Routes: From the North, South and East: Exit the M1 at Junction 36 and follow signs to Sheffield (A61). Continue for 4 miles then take the 3rd exit at the 2nd roundabout into Leppings Lane. The ground is situated on the left; From the West: Take the A57 until the road splits in two. Take the left fork (A6101). After 3¾ miles turn left onto the one-way system and follow the road round to the right onto Holme Lane. This road becomes Bradfield Road. At the junction with the A61 (Penistone Road), turn left towards Barnsley. The stadium is on the left after Hillsborough Park.

SHREWSBURY TOWN FC

Founded: 1886 (**Entered League**: 1950)
Nickname: 'Town'
Ground: Greenhous Meadow Stadium, Oteley Road, Shrewsbury SY2 6ST
Ground Capacity: 9,875 (All seats)
Record Attendance: 18,917 (26th April 1961)
Pitch Size: 116 × 75 yards

Colours: Shirts and shorts are Blue with Amber and White trim
Telephone Nº: (01743) 289177
Ticket Office: (01743) 273943
Fax Number: (01743) 246942
Web Site: www.shrewsburytown.com
E-mail: info@shrewsburytown.co.uk

GENERAL INFORMATION

Car Parking: Limited parking at the stadium – Permit Holders only. Parking restrictions are imposted on matchdays with no parking allowed in the vicinity of the stadium. Visiting fans should use the Park & Ride Scheme – cost £2.00 per person for the return journey – see below
Coach Parking: At the stadium
Nearest Railway Station: Shrewsbury (2½ miles)
Nearest Bus Station: Raven Meadows, Shrewsbury
Club Shop: At the ground
Opening Times: Matchdays and Office Hours
Telephone Nº: (01743) 289177

GROUND INFORMATION

Away Supporters' Entrances & Sections:
North Stand entrances and accommodation

ADMISSION INFO (2012/2013 PRICES)

Adult Seating: £21.00 – £24.00
Child Seating: £5.00 – £13.00
Senior Citizen/Student Seating: £16.00 – £18.00
Note: Tickets are £2.00 cheaper if bought before the day of the match. A range of discounted Family Tickets are also available – please contact the club for further details.
Programme Price: £3.00

DISABLED INFORMATION

Wheelchairs: Spaces in the North, South and East Stands
Helpers: One helper admitted per disabled person
Prices: £13.00 – £15.00 for the disabled (cheaper if bought before the matchday). Helpers are admitted free of charge
Disabled Toilets: Available throughout the ground
Contact: (01743) 273943 (Bookings are necessary)

Travelling Supporters' Information:
Park & Ride information: Buses run every 15 minutes from 12.30pm to 2.30pm on Saturday matchdays and 6.15pm to 7.30pm on matchdays in the week. Parking is free and the return bus journey is £2.00 per person. Buses return to the car parks immediately after the match finishes and car parks will remain open for one hour only. Car Park Locations:
Oxon Park and Ride Site: From the West and North West. At the junction of the A5 and the A458 (Churncote Roundabout) follow the signs A458 'Shrewsbury Town Centre'. Oxon Park and Ride Site is clearly signposted; **The Shirehall**: From all routes proceed along the A5 to Emstrey Island Roundabout into Shrewsbury, take the A5064 along London Road to the Column roundabout. Take the 3rd exit at the roundabout and the first right into the Shirehall Car Park; **Shirehall Overflow Car Park**: Follow directions to London Road as above. Before you reach the roundabout the car park is on the right-hand side. Proceed on foot to the Shirehall main car park for the bus.

SOUTHAMPTON FC

Founded: 1885 (**Entered League**: 1920)
Former Names: Southampton St. Mary's YMCA FC (1885-1897)
Nickname: 'Saints'
Ground: St. Mary's Stadium, Britannia Road, Southampton SO14 5FP
Ground Capacity: 32,689 (All seats)
Record Attendance: 32,151 (29th December 2003)

Pitch Size: 112 × 72 yards
Colours: Red and White shirts with Black shorts
Telephone Nº: 0845 688-9448
Ticket Office: 0845 688-9288
Ticket Office Fax Number: 0845 688-9291
General Fax Number: (023) 8072-7727
Web Site: www.saintsfc.co.uk
E-mail: sfc@saintsfc.co.uk

GENERAL INFORMATION

Car Parking: Park & Ride only – must be pre-booked
Coach Parking: By Police direction
Nearest Railway Station: Southampton Central
Nearest Bus Station: Western Esplanade
Club Shop: At the ground and also at West Quay
Opening Times: Monday to Saturday 9.00am – 5.00pm
Telephone Nº: 0845 688-9433

GROUND INFORMATION

Away Supporters' Entrances & Sections:
Northam Stand

ADMISSION INFO (2012/2013 PRICES)

Matchday admission prices for the 2012/2013 season had not been fixed when we went to press so please contact the club directly for further pricing information.
Programme Price: £3.00

DISABLED INFORMATION

Wheelchairs: 200 spaces in total for Home and Away fans throughout the ground
Helpers: One helper admitted per disabled person
Prices: £10.00 – £20.00 for each disabled supporter. Helpers are admitted free of charge.
Disabled Toilets: Available in all Stands
Contact: (023) 8072-7777 (Bookings are necessary)
E-mail Contact: disability@saintsfc.co.uk

Travelling Supporters' Information:
Routes: Although the ground is situated in the Melbourne Street/Marine Parade area of Southampton, no parking is available in the immediate vicinity except by special arrangement for Disabled supporters. There are a number of well-signposted Park and Ride car parks around the City and those designated for Away fans should be clearly marked.

SOUTHEND UNITED FC

Founded: 1906 (**Entered League**: 1920)
Former Name: Southend Athletic FC
Nickname: 'Shrimpers' 'Blues'
Ground: Roots Hall Ground, Victoria Avenue,
Southend-on-Sea   SS2 6NQ
Ground Capacity: 12,163 (All seats)
Record Attendance: 31,033 (10th January 1979)

Pitch Size: 110 × 74 yards
Colours: Blue shirts with White shorts
Telephone Nº: (01702) 304050
Ticket Office: 08444 770077
Fax Number: (01702) 304124
Web Site: www.southendunited.co.uk
E-mail: info@southend-united.co.uk

GENERAL INFORMATION

Car Parking: Car park at the ground for 450 cars – Season Ticket holders only. Otherwise use street parking
Coach Parking: Car park at the ground. Coach drivers should contact the club prior to the game
Nearest Railway Station: Prittlewell (¼ mile)
Nearest Bus Station: London Road, Southend
Club Shop: At the ground
Opening Times: Monday to Friday and Matchdays during office hours. Non-Match Saturdays 10.00am to 3.00pm
Telephone Nº: (01702) 351117

GROUND INFORMATION

Away Supporters' Entrances & Sections:
North Stand turnstiles for North Stand seating

ADMISSION INFO (2012/2013 PRICES)

Adult Seating: £21.00   (£19.00 purchased in advance)
Young Person Seating: £14.00   (£12.00 in advance)
Junior Seating: £10.00   (Under-8s £5.00)
Student Seating: £14.00   (£12.00 purchased in advance)
Senior Citizen Seating: £15.00   (£13.00 in advance)
Note: Tickets are cheaper when purchased in advance and other discounts are available in the Family Enclosure.
Programme Price: £3.00

DISABLED INFORMATION

Wheelchairs: 20 spaces in total for Home and Away fans in the disabled section, West Stand
Helpers: One helper admitted per disabled person
Prices: Concessionary prices apply to disabled. Helpers receive complimentary tickets
Disabled Toilets: One available in the disabled area
Commentaries are available for the blind
Contact: 08444 770077   (Bookings are necessary)

Travelling Supporters' Information:
Routes: From the North and West: From the M25 take Junction 29 and follow the A127 to Southend. About 1 mile outside of Southend Town Centre, take the 3rd exit at the roundabout into Victoria Avenue for the ground; From the A13: Follow signs for Southend, turn left into West Road at Westcliff. At the end of West Road turn left into Victoria Avenue – the ground is on the left.

STEVENAGE FC

Founded: 1976
Former Names: None
Nickname: 'Boro'
Ground: Lamex Stadium, Broadhall Way, Stevenage, Hertfordshire SG2 8RH
Record Attendance: 8,040 (25th January 1998)
Pitch Size: 110 × 70 yards

Colours: Red and White shirts with Red shorts
Telephone Nº: (01438) 223223
Daytime Phone Nº: (01438) 223223
Fax Number: (01438) 743666
Ground Capacity: 7,104
Seating Capacity: 3,404
Web site: www.stevenagefc.com

GENERAL INFORMATION

Car Parking: Fairlands Show Ground (opposite)
Coach Parking: At the ground
Nearest Railway Station: Stevenage (1 mile)
Nearest Bus Station: Stevenage
Club Shop: At the ground
Opening Times: Tuesday to Thursday and matchdays 10.00am to 5.00pm
Telephone Nº: 0870 811-2494

GROUND INFORMATION

Away Supporters' Entrances & Sections:
South Terrace entrances and accommodation

ADMISSION INFO (2011/2012 PRICES)

Adult Standing: £17.00
Adult Seating: £21.00 – £23.00
Under-21s Standing: £10.00
Under-21s Seating: £14.00 – £16.00
Under-12s Standing: £3.00
Under-12s Seating: £10.00 – £12.00
Concessionary Standing: £15.00
Concessionary Seating: £18.00 – £20.00
Note: Prices vary depending on the category of the game
Programme Price: £3.00

DISABLED INFORMATION

Wheelchairs: 10 spaces available by the North Terrace
Helpers: Admitted
Prices: £9.00 for the disabled. Free of charge for helpers
Disabled Toilets: Yes
Contact: (01438) 223223   (Bookings are necessary)

Travelling Supporters' Information:
Routes: Exit the A1(M) at Junction 7 and take the B197. The ground is on the right at the 2nd roundabout.
Bus Routes: SB4 and SB5

STOKE CITY FC

Founded: 1863 (**Entered League**: 1888)
Former Name: Stoke FC
Nickname: 'The Potters'
Ground: Britannia Stadium, Stanley Matthews Way, Stoke-on-Trent ST4 4EG
Ground Capacity: 27,650 (All seats)
Record Attendance: 28,218 (5th January 2002)

Pitch Size: 110 × 70 yards
Colours: Red and White striped shirts, White shorts
Telephone Nº: 0871 663-2008
Ticket Office: (01782) 367599
Fax Number: (01782) 592210
Web Site: www.stokecityfc.com
E-mail: info@stokecityfc.com

GENERAL INFORMATION

Car Parking: At the ground (bookings necessary). Also various car parks within 10 minutes walk
Coach Parking: At the ground
Nearest Railway Station: Stoke-on-Trent (1½ miles)
Nearest Bus Station: Glebe Street, Stoke-on-Trent
Club Shop: At the ground, at the Potteries Shopping Centre in Hanley and at Roebuck Centre in Newcastle-under-Lyme
Opening Times: Monday to Friday 9.00am – 5.30pm and non-match Saturdays 9.00am – 2.00pm. Saturday Matchdays 9.00am to 2.00pm and Final whistle to 5.30pm. Evening matchdays 9.00am to kick-off and Final whistle to 10.00pm
Telephone Nº: 0871 663-2008

GROUND INFORMATION

Away Supporters' Sections: South Stand

ADMISSION INFO (2011/2012 PRICES)

Adult Seating: £25.00 – £45.00
Under-17s Seating: £15.00 – £24.00
Under-11s Seating: £8.00 – £21.00
Senior Citizen Seating: £19.00 – £32.00
Note: Prices vary depending on the category of the game
Programme Price: £3.00

DISABLED INFORMATION

Wheelchairs: 112 spaces available in total
Helpers: One helper admitted per disabled person
Prices: £19.00 to £32.00 for each disabled fan plus helper
Disabled Toilets: Available
Commentaries are available – phone for details
Contact: 0871 663-2008 (Bookings are necessary)

Travelling Supporters' Information:
Routes: From the North, South and West: Exit the M6 at Junction 15 and take the A500 to Stoke-on-Trent then the A50 towards Derby/Uttoxeter (the Britannia Stadium is signposted and visible to the right). Once on the A50 take the fist exit, turn right at the traffic lights and cross over the flyover. Turn right at the first roundabout, left at the next roundabout and right at the third roundabout for the stadium; From the East: Take the A50 to Stoke-on-Trent and take the last turn-off (signposted for Britannia Stadium). Go straight on at the first roundabout then right at the second roundabout to reach the stadium.

SUNDERLAND AFC

Founded: 1879 (**Entered League**: 1890)
Former Names: Sunderland and District Teachers FC
Nickname: 'The Black Cats'
Ground: Stadium of Light, Sunderland   SR5 1SU
Ground Capacity: 49,000 (All seats)
Record Attendance: 48,355 (13th April 2002)
Pitch Size: 110 × 74 yards (101 × 68 metres)

Colours: Red and White striped shirts, Black shorts
Telephone Nº: 0871 911-1200
Ticket Office: 0871 911-1973
Fax Number: (0191) 551-5123
Web Site: www.safc.com
E-mail: enquiries@safc.com

GENERAL INFORMATION

Car Parking: Spaces for 1,100 cars (reserved)
Coach Parking: At the ground
Nearest Railway Station: Sunderland (1 mile)
Nearest Bus Station: Town Centre (1 mile)
Club Shop: At the Stadium, plus smaller stores in Sainsburys in Washington and Debenhams in Sunderland
Opening Times: Monday to Saturday 9.00am – 5.00pm
Telephone Nº: 0871 911-1200

GROUND INFORMATION

Away Supporters' Entrances & Sections:
South Stand

ADMISSION INFO (2011/2012 PRICES)

Adult Seating: £25.00 – £35.00
Under-16s: £10.00 – £13.00 (some sections only)
Senior Citizen/Under-22s Seating: £18.00 – £23.00
Note: Prices vary depending on the category of the game.
Programme Price: £3.00

DISABLED INFORMATION

Wheelchairs: 180 spaces in total throughout the stadium
Helpers: Admitted
Prices: Normal prices for the disabled. Free for helpers
Disabled Toilets: Available in all stands and Corporate areas
Contact: 0845 671-1973   (Bookings are necessary)

Travelling Supporters' Information:
Routes: From All Parts: Exit the A1 at the A690 Durham/Sunderland exit. After approximately 4 miles turn left onto the A19 (signposted Tyne Tunnel). Keep in the left lane and take the slip road (signposted Washington/Sunderland) onto the bridge over the River Wear. Turn right onto the A1231 (signposted Washington/Sunderland), stay on this road going straight across 4 roundabouts into Sunderland. Continue straight through 2 sets of traffic lights and the Stadium car park is on the right, about 1 mile past the traffic lights.

SWANSEA CITY FC

Founded: 1912 (**Entered League**: 1920)
Former Name: Swansea Town FC (1912-1970)
Nickname: 'The Swans'
Ground: Liberty Stadium, Landore, Swansea, SA1 2FA
Ground Capacity: 20,532 (All seats)
Record Attendance: 32,796 (at the Vetch Field)

Pitch Size: 115 × 74 yards
Colours: All White shirts, shorts and socks
Telephone Nº: (01792) 616600
Ticket Office: 0844 815-6665
Fax Number: (01792) 616606
Web Site: www.swanseacity.net
E-mail: info@swanseacityfc.co.uk

GENERAL INFORMATION

Car Parking: Reserved parking only at the stadium but 3,000 spaces are available in a Park & Ride scheme just off Junction 45 of the M4.
Coach Parking: By Police direction
Nearest Railway Station: Swansea High Street (1½ miles)
Nearest Bus Station: Quadrant Depot (2½ miles)
Club Shop: At the ground
Opening Times: Monday to Saturday 9.00am – 5.00pm
Telephone Nº: 0871 222-3434

GROUND INFORMATION

Away Supporters' Entrances & Sections:
North Stand

ADMISSION INFO (2011/2012 PRICES)

Adult Seating: £35.00
Under-16s Seating: £17.50
Senior Citizen Seating: £17.50
Student Seating: £17.50
Programme Price: £3.00

DISABLED INFORMATION

Wheelchairs: 250 spaces available in total for Home and Away fans together with 250 spaces for helpers
Helpers: One helper admitted per wheelchair
Prices: Normal prices apply for the disabled. Free for helpers
Disabled Toilets: Available
There are a number of disabled parking spaces available at the stadium
Contact: (01792) 616402   (Bookings are necessary)

Travelling Supporters' Information:
Routes: From All Parts: Exit the M4 at Junction 45 and follow signs for Swansea (A4067). The stadium is clearly signposted.

SWINDON TOWN FC

Founded: 1881 (**Entered League**: 1920)
Nickname: 'Robins'
Ground: County Ground, County Road, Swindon, SN1 2ED
Ground Capacity: 14,983 (All seats)
Record Attendance: 32,000 (15th January 1972)
Pitch Size: 110 × 73 yards

Colours: Red shirts and shorts
Telephone Nº: 0871 876-1879
Ticket Office: 0871 876-1993
Fax Number: 0844 880-1112
Web Site: www.swindontownfc.co.uk
E-mail: boxoffice@swindontownfc.co.uk

GENERAL INFORMATION

Car Parking: Town Centre
Coach Parking: Car park adjacent to the ground
Nearest Railway Station: Swindon (½ mile)
Nearest Bus Station: Swindon (½ mile)
Club Shop: The Swindon Town Superstore
Opening Times: Weekdays 9.00am – 5.00pm, Non-Matchday Saturdays 9.00am – 12.00pm and Saturday Matchdays 9.00am to 3.00pm
Telephone Nº: 0871 876-1969

GROUND INFORMATION

Away Supporters' Entrances & Sections:
Arkell's Stand turnstiles for the Stratton Bank

ADMISSION INFO (2012/2013 PRICES)

Adult Seating: £19.00 – £25.00
Junior Seating: £12.00 (Under-10s admitted free of charge)
Concessionary Seating: £15.00 – £19.00
Young Adult Seating: £15.00 – £17.00
Note: A range of Family Tickets are also available
Programme Price: £3.00

DISABLED INFORMATION

Wheelchairs: 56 spaces in total for Home and Away fans in disabled section, in front of Arkell's Stand
Helpers: One helper admitted per wheelchair disabled fan
Prices: £12.00–£17.00 for each disabled fan and their helper
Disabled Toilets: Available within the disabled area
Commentaries are available for the blind
Contact: 0871 876-1993   (Bookings are necessary)

Travelling Supporters' Information:
Routes: From London, the East and the South: Exit the M4 at Junction 15 and take the A345 into Swindon along Queen's Drive. Take the 3rd exit at 'Magic Roundabout' into County Road; From the West: Exit the M4 at Junction 15 then as above; From the North: Take the M4 or A345/A420/A361 to the County Road roundabout, then as above.

TORQUAY UNITED FC

Founded: 1899   (**First Entered League**: 1927)
Former Name: Torquay Town FC (1899-1910)
Nickname: 'Gulls'
Ground: Plainmoor Ground, Torquay   TQ1 3PS
Ground Capacity: 6,196   **Seating Capacity**: 2,750
Record Attendance: 21,908 (29th January 1955)
Pitch Size: 112 × 72 yards

Colours: Shirts are Yellow with Royal Blue trim, shorts and socks are Yellow
Telephone Nº: (01803) 328666 (Option 0)
Ticket Office: (01803) 328666
Fax Number: (01803) 323976
Web Site: www.torquayunited.com
E-mail: reception@torquayunited.com

GENERAL INFORMATION
Car Parking: Street parking
Coach Parking: Lymington Road Coach Station (½ mile)
Nearest Railway Station: Torquay (2 miles)
Nearest Bus Station: Lymington Road (½ mile)
Club Shop: At the ground
Opening Times: Matchdays and during Office Hours
Telephone Nº: (01803) 328666

GROUND INFORMATION
Away Supporters' Entrances & Sections:
Babbacombe End turnstiles for Babbacombe End

ADMISSION INFO (2012/2013 PRICES)
Adult Standing: £17.00
Adult Seating: £19.00 – £20.00
Concessionary Standing: £13.00
Concessionary Seating: £15.00 – £16.00
Under-16s Standing/Seating: £6.00
Programme Price: £3.00

DISABLED INFORMATION
Wheelchairs: 10 spaces in front of Ellacombe End Stand for home supporters plus 5 spaces in the Away end.
Helpers: One helper admitted per wheelchair
Prices: Normal prices for the disabled. Free for helpers
Disabled Toilets: Available in the Ellacombe End and the Away End
Audio facilities are available for the blind
Contact: (01803) 328666 (Bookings necessary for the blind)

Travelling Supporters' Information:
Routes: From the North and East: Take the M5 to the A38 then A380 to Torquay. On entering Torquay, turn left at the 1st set of traffic lights after Riviera Way Retail Park into Hele Road. Following signs for the ground, continue straight on over two mini-roundabouts, go up West Hill Road to the traffic lights, then straight ahead into Warbro Road. The ground is situated on the right after 200 yards.

TOTTENHAM HOTSPUR FC

Founded: 1882 (**Entered League**: 1908)
Former Name: Hotspur FC (1882-1884)
Nickname: 'Spurs'
Ground: White Hart Lane, Bill Nicholson Way,
748 High Road, Tottenham, London   N17 0AP
Ground Capacity: 36,240 (All seats)
Record Attendance: 75,038 (5th March 1938)

Pitch Size: 110 × 73 yards
Colours: White shirts with Navy Blue shorts
Telephone N°: 0844 499-5000
Ticket Office: 0844 844-0102
Fax Number: (020) 8365-5175
Web Site: www.tottenhamhotspur.com
E-mail: email@tottenhamhotspur.com

GENERAL INFORMATION

Car Parking: None within ¼ mile of the ground
Coach Parking: Northumberland Park, West Road
Nearest Railway Station: White Hart Lane (nearby) or
Northumberland Park
Nearest Tube Station: Seven Sisters (Victoria Line) or
Manor House (Piccadilly Line)
Club Shop: Megastore at the ground plus stores in Harlow,
Enfield and Chelmsford
Opening Times: Monday to Saturday 9.30am – 5.30pm
(open from 10.00am on Monday and Tuesday). Also Sundays
10.00am – 4.00pm
Telephone N°: 0844 499-5000

GROUND INFORMATION

Away Supporters' Entrances & Sections:
Park Lane entrances for South Stand

ADMISSION INFO (2012/2013 PRICES)

Adult Seating: £32.00 – £81.00
Child Seating: £17.00 – £28.00
Senior Citizen Seating: £19.00 – £31.00
Note: Additional discounts are available for members and
prices vary depending on the category of the game
Programme Price: £3.50

DISABLED INFORMATION

Wheelchairs: 70 spaces for home fans, 8 for away fans in
the disabled areas. This comprises 51 wheelchair spaces
(46 for home fans and 5 for away fans) plus 27 ambulant
spaces (24 homes fans and 3 for away fans).
Home supporters area: North Stand West Lower Tier and
South Lower; Away Supporters area: South Stand Lower Tier.
Helpers: One helper admitted per disabled person
Prices: £30.00 – £67.50 for the disabled (£17.50 for
Concessions). Helpers are admitted free of charge
Disabled Toilets: 4 available in the North Stand and 2
available in the South Stand
Contact: (020) 8365-5161   (Bookings are necessary)

Travelling Supporters' Information:
Routes: From All Parts: Take the A406 North Circular to Edmonton and at traffic lights follow signs for Tottenham (A1010) into
Fore Street for the ground.

TRANMERE ROVERS FC

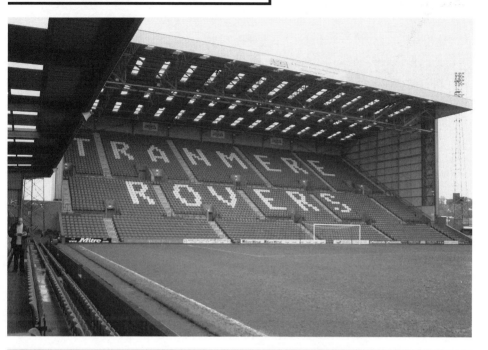

Founded: 1884 (**Entered League**: 1921)
Former Name: Belmont FC
Nickname: 'Rovers'
Ground: Prenton Park, Prenton Road West, Birkenhead CH42 9PY
Ground Capacity: 16,151 (All seats)
Record Attendance: 24,424 (5th February 1972)

Pitch Size: 110 × 70 yards
Colours: White shirts and shorts
Telephone Nº: 0871 221-2001
Ticket Office: 0871 221-2001
Fax Number: (0151) 609-0606
Web Site: www.tranmererovers.co.uk
E-mail: info@tranmererovers.co.uk

GENERAL INFORMATION

Car Parking: Large car park at the ground (£5.00 per car)
Coach Parking: At the ground (£10.00 charge)
Nearest Railway Stations: Hamilton Square, Rock Ferry and Conway Park (approximately 1½ miles)
Nearest Bus Station: Conway Park (Town Centre)
Club Shop: At the ground
Opening Times: Weekdays 9.30am–5.00pm, Matchdays 10.00am– kick-off, non-Saturday matchdays 10.00am–1.00pm
Telephone Nº: 0871 221-2001

GROUND INFORMATION

Away Supporters' Entrances & Sections:
Cowshed Stand turnstiles 5-9 – access from Borough Road (Away section capacity: 2,500)

ADMISSION INFO (2012/2013 PRICES)

Adult Seating: £14.50 – £23.50
Child Seating: £6.00
Concessionary Seating (Seniors 60+): £10.00 – £12.00
Young Persons Ticket (Ages 17-22): £10.00 – £15.00
Programme Price: £3.00
Note: Young Person tickets must be purchased from the Ticket Office prior to the game and are only sold upon presentation of photographic proof of age.

DISABLED INFORMATION

Wheelchairs: 28 spaces in total for Home and Away fans in the disabled section, Bebington Paddock
Helpers: One helper admitted per disabled person
Prices: £6.50
Disabled Toilets: 2 available in the disabled section
Contact: 0871 221-2001 (Bookings are necessary)

Travelling Supporters' Information:
Routes: From the North: Take the Mersey Tunnel (Queensway), bear right onto the flyover after the tollbooths and continue on to Borough Road. Continue on Borough Road for approximately 1 mile and the ground is situated on the right; From the South and East: Exit the M53 at Junction 4 and take the 3rd exit at roundabout (B5151). After 2½ miles turn right into Prenton Road West for the ground.

WALSALL FC

Founded: 1888 (**Entered League**: 1892)
Former Name: Walsall Town Swifts FC (1888-1895)
Nickname: 'Saddlers'
Ground: Banks's Stadium, Bescot Crescent, Walsall,
West Midlands   WS1 4SA
Ground Capacity: 11,300 (All seats)
Record Attendance: 11,049 (9th May 2004)
Pitch Size: 110 × 73 yards

Colours: Red shirts with White shorts
Telephone Nº: (01922) 622791
Ticket Office: (01922) 651416 or (01922) 651414
Fax Number: (01922) 613202
Web Site: www.saddlers.co.uk
E-mail: info@walsallfc.co.uk

GENERAL INFORMATION

Car Parking: Car park at the ground
Coach Parking: At the ground
Nearest Railway Station: Bescot (adjacent)
Nearest Bus Station: Bradford Place, Walsall
Club Shop: At the ground and in Bradford Street, Walsall
Opening Times: Weekdays and Matchdays 9.00am–5.00pm
Telephone Nº: (01922) 631072 (Bradford Street)

GROUND INFORMATION

Away Supporters' Entrances & Sections:
Turnstiles 21-28 for Dains Stand accommodation

ADMISSION INFO (2012/2013 PRICES)

Adult Seating: £16.50 – £23.50
Child Seating: £8.50 – £13.50
Concessionary Seating: £11.50 – £17.50
Note: Discounts are available for advance bookings and
prices vary depending on the category of the game.
Savings from Family Tickets are available in some stands
Programme Price: £2.50

DISABLED INFORMATION

Wheelchairs: 30 spaces in total for Home and Away fans in
the disabled section, Walsall Bite Size Stand
Helpers: One helper admitted per disabled person
Prices: £21.50 for the wheelchair disabled. Helpers are
admitted free of charge
Disabled Toilets: Adjacent to disabled viewing bays
A special Lounge for fans with disabilities is available
Contact: (01922) 651416   (Bookings are necessary)

Travelling Supporters' Information:
Routes: From All Parts: Exit the M6 at Junction 9 turning North towards Walsall onto the A461. After ¼ mile turn right into
Wallows Lane and pass over the railway bridge. Then take the 1st right into Bescot Crescent and the ground is ½ mile along on
the left adjacent to Bescot Railway Station.

WATFORD FC

Founded: 1881 (**Entered League**: 1920)
Former Names: Formed by the amalgamation of West Herts FC and St. Mary's FC
Nickname: 'Hornets'
Ground: Vicarage Road Stadium, Watford, WD18 0ER
Ground Capacity: 17,598 (All seats)
Record Attendance: 34,099 (3rd February 1969)

Pitch Size: 114 × 73 yards
Colours: Yellow shirts with Red shorts
Telephone N°: 0844 856-1881
Ticket Office: 0844 856-1881
Fax Number: (01923) 496001
Web Site: www.watfordfc.com
E-mail: yourvoice@watfordfc.com

GENERAL INFORMATION

Car Parking: Nearby multi-storey car parks and schools
Coach Parking: By Police direction
Nearest Railway Station: Watford Junction or Watford Tube Station (Metropolitan Line)
Nearest Bus Station: Watford Town Centre
Club Shop: The Hornets Shop at Vicarage Road Stadium
Opening Times: Monday to Saturday 9.00am to 5.30pm
Telephone N°: 0844 856-1881

GROUND INFORMATION

Away Supporters' Entrances & Sections:
Vicarage Road End entrances and accommodation

ADMISSION INFO (2012/2013 PRICES)

Adult Seating: £10.00 – £30.00
Child Seating: £1.00 – £10.00
Senior Citizen Seating: £10.00 – £18.00
Note: Certain matches are designated as Special Family Day events and lower prices apply for these games.
Programme Price: £3.00

DISABLED INFORMATION

Wheelchairs: 41 spaces in total in the disabled sections, South East Corner, North East Corner and South West Corner
Helpers: One helper admitted per disabled person
Prices: £10.00 – £25.00 for the disabled. Middle to high rate disability documentation must be provided when booking.
Disabled Toilets: Adjacent to disabled enclosures
Commentaries available around the ground – no charge
Contact: 0844 856-1881 (Bookings in advance helpful)

Travelling Supporters' Information:
Routes: From the North: Exit the M1 at Junction 5 and take the new road (A4008) towards Watford Town Centre. This will take you around the ring road, follow signs for Watford General Hospital. The ground is next to the hospital; From the South: Exit M1 at Junction 5 (then as North); From the East: Exit the M25 at Junction 21A and join the M1 at Junction 6. Exit at Junction 5 (then as North); From the West: Exit the M25 at Junction 19 and take the third exit off the roundabout onto the A411 (Hempstead Road) signposted for Watford. Continue for approximately two miles and go straight on at the roundabout (enter the right-hand lane) for the next roundabout and take the third exit into Rickmansworth Road. Take the second turning on the left into Cassio Road. Go through the traffic lights into Merton Road and follow signs for Watford General Hospital into Vicarage Road.

WEST BROMWICH ALBION FC

Founded: 1879 (**Entered League**: 1888)
Former Name: West Bromwich Strollers (1879-1880)
Nickname: 'Throstles' 'Baggies' 'Albion'
Ground: The Hawthorns, Halfords Lane,
West Bromwich, West Midlands   B71 4LF
Ground Capacity: 26,484 (All seats)
Record Attendance: 64,815 (6th March 1937)

Pitch Size: 115 × 74 yards
Colours: Navy Blue & White striped shirts, White shorts
Telephone Nº: 0871 271-1100
Ticket Office: 0871 271-9780
Fax Number: 0871 271-9861
Web Site: www.wba.co.uk
E-mail: enquiries@wbafc.co.uk

GENERAL INFORMATION

Car Parking: Halfords Lane Car Parks, East Stand Car Park and several independent car parks
Coach Parking: At the ground
Nearest Railway Station: Hawthorns (200 yards) or Rolfe Street, Smethwick (1½ miles)
Nearest Midland Metro: Hawthorns (200 yards)
Nearest Bus Station: West Bromwich Town Centre
Club Shop: At the ground and at the Merry Hill Centre
Opening Times: Weekdays 9.00am – 5.00pm and Saturday Matchdays 9.00am – 2.45pm
Telephone Nº: 0871 271-9790

GROUND INFORMATION

Away Supporters' Entrances & Sections:
Smethwick End 'A' turnstiles

ADMISSION INFO (2012/2013 PRICES)

Adult Seating: £25.00 – £40.00
Child Seating: £10.00 – £20.00
Senior Citizen Seating: £15.00 – £25.00
Student Seating: £15.00 – £25.00
Programme Price: £3.00

DISABLED INFORMATION

Wheelchairs: 150 spaces in total in the disabled sections, Birmingham Road End, Smethwick End and the East Stand
Helpers: One helper admitted per disabled person (subject to availability of space)
Prices: £10.00 – £22.00 for the disabled. Free for helpers
Disabled Toilets: Available within disabled section
Contact: 0871 271-1100 (Bookings are necessary)

Travelling Supporters' Information:
Routes: From All Parts: Exit the M5 at Junction 1 and follow Matchday signs for the ground. The matchday traffic plan has made the "obvious" route via the A41 unusable for home games.

WEST HAM UNITED FC

Founded: 1895 (**Entered League**: 1919)
Former Name: Thames Iron Works FC
Nickname: 'Hammers'
Ground: Boleyn Ground, Green Street, Upton Park, London   E13 9AZ
Ground Capacity: 35,303 (All seats)
Record Attendance: 42,322 (17th October 1970)

Pitch Size: 110 × 70 yards
Colours: Claret and Blue shirts with White shorts
Telephone Nº: (020) 8548-2748
Ticket Office: 0871 222-7000
Fax Number: (020) 8548-2758
Web Site: www.whufc.com
E-mail: customerservices@westhamunited.co.uk

GENERAL INFORMATION

Car Parking: Street parking
Coach Parking: By Police direction
Nearest Railway Station: Barking
Nearest Tube Station: Upton Park (5 minutes walk)
Club Shops: At the Stadium and also at Lakeside
Opening Times: Weekdays and Matchdays 9.30am–5.00pm
Telephone Nº: (020) 8548-2794 (Stadium Store);
(01708) 890258 (Lakeside Store)
Mail-Order Nº: 0870 112-2700

GROUND INFORMATION

Away Supporters' Entrances & Sections:
Priory Road entrance for the Centenary Stand

ADMISSION INFO (2012/2013 PRICES)

Adult Seating: £49.00 – £67.00
Under-16s Seating: £21.00 – £35.00
Senior Citizen/Concessionary Seating: £21.00 – £35.00
Note: Prices vary depending on the category of the game and discounts are available to members for some games
Programme Price: £3.00

DISABLED INFORMATION

Wheelchairs: 150 spaces for home fans, 12 spaces for away fans in the disabled area, Centenary Stand
Helpers: Admitted
Prices: £18.00 – £21.00 for the disabled. Free for helpers
Disabled Toilets: 12 available
Contact: Gina Allen (020) 8548-2725 (Bookings necessary)

Travelling Supporters' Information:
Routes: From the North and West: Take the North Circular (A406) to the A124 (East Ham) then along Barking Road for approximately 1½ miles until approaching the traffic lights at the crossroad. Turn right into Green Street, the ground is on the right-hand side; From the South: Take the Blackwall Tunnel and the A13 to Canning Town. Follow signs for East Ham (A124). After 1¾ miles turn left into Green Street; From the East: Take the A13 and turn right onto the A117 at the crossroads. After approximately 1 mile turn left at the crossroads onto the A124. Turn right after ¾ mile into Green Street for the ground.

WIGAN ATHLETIC FC

Founded: 1932 (**Entered League**: 1978)
Nickname: 'Latics'
Ground: DW Stadium, Robin Park, Newtown, Wigan, Lancashire   WN5 0UZ
Ground Capacity: 25,133 (All seats)
Record Attendance: 25,133 (11th May 2008)
Pitch Size: 115 × 74 yards

Colours: Blue and White striped shirts, Blue shorts
Telephone Nº: (01942) 774000
Ticket Office: 0871 66-33-552
Fax Number: (01942) 770477
Web Site: www.wiganathletic.com
E-mail: info@wiganathletic.com

GENERAL INFORMATION

Car Parking: 2,500 spaces available at the ground (£4.00 for cars, £10.00 for minibuses, £20.00 for coaches)
Coach Parking: At the ground
Nearest Railway Station: Wallgate and Wigan North Western (1 mile)
Nearest Bus Station: Wigan
Club Shop: At the DW Stadium (matchdays only) and also a store in Wigan Town Centre.
Opening Times: Weekdays 9.00am to 5.00pm and Matchdays 10.00am – 4.00pm

GROUND INFORMATION
Away Supporters' Entrances & Sections:
North Stand entrances and accommodation

ADMISSION INFO (2012/2013 PRICES)
Adult Seating: £20.00 – £30.00
Child/Senior Citizen Seating: £15.00 – £20.00
Team Latics: £5.00 – £10.00 (Children only)
Note: Prices vary depending on the category of the game
Programme Price: £3.00

DISABLED INFORMATION
Wheelchairs: 25 spaces available in each stand
Helpers: One helper admitted per disabled supporter
Prices: £15.00 – £20.00 for each disabled fan + a helper
Disabled Toilets: Available in every stand
Contact: (01942) 774000   (Bookings are necessary)

Travelling Supporters' Information:
Routes: From North: Exit M6 at Junction 27, turn left at end of slip road then right at T-junction, signposted Shevington. After 1 mile turn left at the mini-roundabout into Old Lane (B5375). After approx. 2 miles winding through countryside turn right at traffic lights into Scot Lane. Stadium is next left; From South & West: Exit M6 at Junction 25 follow signs for Wigan (A49). After approx. 2 miles a complex junction is reached, keep in left-hand lane (McDonalds on right). Turn left at traffic light filter lane into Robin Park Road. Turn right at third set of traffic lights and follow road to stadium; From East: Exit M61 Junction 6, take 1st exit at roundabout. At next roundabout take 1st left into Chorley Road. Follow signs for Wigan B5238, first turning right then left at Aspull Roundabout. After 2 miles turn right at traffic lights after Earl of Balcarres Pub to face Tesco. Turn left at lights, keep in left lane turn left at next lights with the Quality Hotel on the corner. Follow ring road, get into second lane from right as road bears right into Caroline Street, signposted Orrell. Continue on ring road as it bears left passing B&Q on left, pass Wigan Pier on right and as road goes under railway bridge get into right hand lane to turn right at lights into Robin Park Road. Then South & West.

WOLVERHAMPTON WANDERERS FC

Founded: 1877 (**Entered League**: 1888)
Former Names: Formed by the amalgamation of St. Luke's FC and The Wanderers Football & Cricket Club in 1879. St. Luke's is considered the start of the club
Nickname: 'Wolves'
Ground: Molineux Stadium, Waterloo Road, Wolverhampton WV1 4QR
Ground Capacity: 31,500

Record Attendance: 61,315 (11th February 1939)
Pitch Size: 110 × 75 yards
Colours: Gold shirts with Black shorts
Telephone Nº: 0871 222-2220
Ticket Office: 0871 222-1877
Fax Number: (01902) 687006
Web Site: www.wolves.co.uk
E-mail: info@wolves.co.uk

GENERAL INFORMATION

Car Parking: Around West Park, Newhampton Road and rear of the Stan Cullis Stand. Also in City Centre (5 minutes walk)
Coach Parking: By Police direction
Nearest Railway Station: Wolverhampton (¾ mile)
Nearest Bus Station: Wolverhampton (¾ mile)
Club Shop: At the ground and in the City Centre
Opening Times: Daily from 9.00am – 5.00pm
Telephone Nº: 0871 222-2220

GROUND INFORMATION

Away Supporters' Entrances & Sections:
Jack Harris turnstiles for Block 5 or Steve Bull Stand Lower Tier (turnstiles for Block 3)

ADMISSION INFO (2011/2012 PRICES)

Adult Seating: £24.00 – £40.00
Senior Citizen Seating: £14.00 – £28.00
Under-17s Seating: £11.00 – £20.00
Under-12s Seating: £8.00 – £17.00
Programme Price: £3.00

DISABLED INFORMATION

Wheelchairs: 104 spaces in total in the disabled sections, Stan Cullis Stand and Billy Wright Family Enclosure
Helpers: Admitted
Prices: Please contact the club for details
Disabled Toilets: At both ends of the Stan Cullis Stand
Contact: 0870 442-0123 (Vicky Goodall)
(Bookings are necessary)

Travelling Supporters' Information:
Routes: From North: Exit M6 Junction 12. At island take 3rd exit onto A5 for Wolverhampton. At next island turn left onto A449. After 6 miles A449 passes under M54, carry straight on and at 6th roundabout (Five Ways) take 3rd exit into Waterloo Road. Molineux is 1 mile straight on; From South West: Exit M5 Junction 2, follow signs for Wolverhampton on A4123 for 8 miles to ring road. Turn left on ring road (follow Molineux Centre signs). Take 2nd exit at next 2 islands * Pass Bank's Brewery and Swimming Baths on left and turn left at next set of traffic lights. Molineux is 500 yards on right; From South/East: Exit M6 Junction 10, take A454 (via Willenhall) to Wolverhampton ring road. At first ring road island take 4th exit (A449 to Stafford). Straight on at next 2 sets of traffic lights. Filter right at third set of lights (Waterloo Road). Molineux is 500 yards on right; From West: Take A41 to Wolverhampton ring road roundabout. Turn left into the ring road. Then as from the South West *

WYCOMBE WANDERERS FC

Founded: 1887 (**Entered League**: 1993)
Nickname: 'The Blues' 'The Chairboys'
Ground: Adams Park, Hillbottom Road, Sands, High Wycombe   HP12 4HJ
Ground Capacity: 10,000
Seating Capacity: 8,250
Record Attendance: 9,971 (10th January 2007)

Pitch Size: 115 × 75 yards
Colours: Navy and Light Blue quarters with Navy shorts
Telephone Nº: (01494) 472100
Ticket Office: (01494) 441118
Fax Number: (01494) 527633
Web Site: www.wwfc.com
E-mail: wwfc@wwfc.com

GENERAL INFORMATION

Car Parking: Car park at the ground
Coach Parking: Car park at the ground
Nearest Railway Station: High Wycombe
Nearest Bus Station: High Wycombe
Club Shop: At the ground and in the Eden Shopping Centre
Opening Times: Matchdays only at the ground and daily at the store in the Eden Shopping Centre
Telephone Nº: (01494) 472100

GROUND INFORMATION

Away Supporters' Entrances & Sections:
Dreams Stand (seating only)

ADMISSION INFO (2012/2013 PRICES)

Adult Standing: £18.00   **Adult Seating**: £20.00–£25.00
Under-16s Standing: £7.00
Under-16s Seating: £7.00 – £18.00
Senior Citizen Standing: £15.00   **Seating**: £18–£20
Student Standing: £13.00   **Seating**: £17.00 – £19.00
Note: A £2.00 discount is available for Blues cardholders
Programme Price: £3.00

DISABLED INFORMATION

Wheelchairs: 50 spaces in total available in the disabled section of the Family Stand and Away Stand
Helpers: One helper admitted per wheelchair
Prices: Full price for the disabled. Free of charge for helpers
Disabled Toilets: Available in the Family Stand
Commentaries are available for 5 people
Contact: (01494) 441118   (Bookings are not necessary)

Travelling Supporters' Information:
Routes: From All Parts: Exit the M40 at Junction 4 and take the A4010 following Aylesbury signs. Go straight on at 3 mini-roundabouts then bear sharp left at the 4th roundabout into Lane End Road. Fork right into Hillbottom Road at the next roundabout. The ground is at the end of the road. Hillbottom Road is on the Sands Industrial Estate; From the Town Centre: Take the A40 West and after 1½ miles turn left into Chapel Lane (after the traffic lights). Turn right then right again at the mini-roundabout into Lane End Road – then as above.

YEOVIL TOWN FC

Founded: 1895
Former Names: Yeovil & Petters United FC
Nickname: 'Glovers'
Ground: Huish Park Stadium, Lufton Way, Yeovil, Somerset   BA22 8YF
Ground Capacity: 9,565 **Seating Capacity**: 5,309
Record Attendance: 9,527 (25th April 2008)

Pitch Size: 108 × 67 yards
Colours: Green and White shirts with Green shorts
Telephone Nº: (01935) 423662
Ticket Office Nº: (01935) 847888
Fax Number: (01935) 473956
Web site: www.ytfc.net
E-mail: info@ytfc.net

GENERAL INFORMATION

Car Parking: Spaces for 1,000 cars at the ground
Coach Parking: At the ground
Nearest Railway Station: Yeovil Pen Mill (2½ miles) and Yeovil Junction (3½ miles)
Nearest Bus Station: Yeovil (2 miles)
Club Shop: At the ground
Opening Times: Weekdays 10.00am – 4.00pm and Matchdays 10.00am – 3.00pm
Telephone Nº: (01935) 423662

GROUND INFORMATION

Away Supporters' Entrances & Sections:
Copse Road End (turnstiles 13-16) and Cowlin Stand (turnstile 12)

ADMISSION INFO (2012/2013 PRICES)

Adult Standing: £17.00 – £19.00
Adult Seating: £17.00 – £22.00
Under-16s Standing: £6.00   **Seating**: £6.00–£7.00
Ages 16 to 21 Standing/Seating: £10.00–£12.00
Senior Citizen Standing: £12.00 – £14.00
Senior Citizen Seating: £13.00 – £19.00
Note: Discounted prices are available for tickets which are purchased in advance.
Programme Price: £3.00

DISABLED INFORMATION

Wheelchairs: 15 spaces for home fans, 5 spaces for away fans
Helpers: Admitted free of charge
Prices: Please phone the club for information
Disabled Toilets: Two are available
Contact: (01935) 847888   (Bookings are recommended)

Travelling Supporters' Information:
Routes: From London: Take the M3 and A303 to Cartgate Roundabout. Enter Yeovil on the A3088. Exit left at the 1st roundabout then straight over the next two roundabouts into Western Avenue. Cross the next roundabout then turn left into Copse Road, where supporters' parking is sited; From the North: Exit the M5 at Junction 25 and take the A358 (Ilminster) and A303 (Eastbound) entering Yeovil on the A3088. Then as above.

YORK CITY FC

Founded: 1922   (**Re-entered League**: 2012)
Nickname: 'The Minstermen'
Ground: Bootham Crescent, York   YO30 7AQ
Ground Capacity: 8,105
Seating Capacity: 3,509
Record Attendance: 28,123 (5th March 1938)
Pitch Size: 115 × 74 yards

Colours: Red shirts with Blue shorts
Telephone Nº: (01904) 624447
Ticket Office: (01904) 624447 Extension 1
Fax Number: (01904) 631457 or 08712 515800
Web Site: www.yorkcityfootballclub.co.uk
E-mail: enquiries@yorkcityfootballclub.co.uk

GENERAL INFORMATION

Car Parking: Street parking
Coach Parking: By Police direction
Nearest Railway Station: York (1 mile)
Club Shop: At the ground
Opening Times: Weekdays 10.30am – 2.30pm and
Saturday Matchdays 1.00pm–3.00pm and 4.40pm–5.30pm;
Evening matches open from 6.00pm
Telephone Nº: (01904) 624447 Extension 4

GROUND INFORMATION

Away Supporters' Entrances & Sections:
Grosvenor Road turnstiles for Grosvenor Road End

ADMISSION INFO (2012/2013 PRICES)

Adult Standing: £15.00 – £19.00
Adult Seating: £16.00 – £19.00
Concessionary Standing: £10.00
Concessionary Seating: £10.00 – £17.00
Under-16s Standing/Seating: £7.00 – £12.00
Programme Price: £3.00

DISABLED INFORMATION

Wheelchairs: 18 spaces in total for Home and Away fans in
the disabled section, in front of the Pitchside Bar
Helpers: One helper admitted per disabled person
Prices: £6.00 – £16.00 for the disabled. Helpers are
admitted free of charge
Disabled Toilets: Available at entrance to the disabled area
Contact: (01904) 624447 (Ext. 1) (Bookings not necessary)

Travelling Supporters' Information:
Routes: From the North: Take the A1 then the A59 following signs for York. Cross the railway bridge and turn left after 2 miles into Water End. Turn right at the end following City Centre signs for nearly ½ mile then turn left into Bootham Crescent; From the South: Take the A64 and turn left after Buckles Inn onto the Outer Ring Road. Turn right onto the A19, follow City Centre signs for 1½ miles then turn left into Bootham Crescent; From the East: Take the Outer Ring Road turning left onto the A19. Then as from the South; From the West: Take the Outer Ring Road turning right onto the A19. Then as from the South.

F.A. Premier League 2011/2012 Season	Arsenal	Aston Villa	Blackburn Rovers	Bolton Wanderers	Chelsea	Everton	Fulham	Liverpool	Manchester City	Manchester United	Newcastle United	Norwich City	Queen's Park Rangers	Stoke City	Sunderland	Swansea City	Tottenham Hotspur	West Bromwich Albion	Wigan Athletic	Wolverhampton Wanderers
Arsenal	■	3-0	7-1	3-0	0-0	1-0	1-1	0-2	1-0	1-2	2-1	3-3	1-0	3-1	2-1	1-0	5-2	3-0	1-2	1-1
Aston Villa	1-2	■	3-1	1-2	2-4	1-1	1-0	0-2	0-1	0-1	1-1	3-2	2-2	1-1	0-0	0-2	1-1	1-2	2-0	0-0
Blackburn Rovers	4-3	1-1	■	1-2	0-1	0-1	3-1	2-3	0-4	0-2	0-2	2-0	3-2	1-2	2-0	4-2	1-2	1-2	0-1	1-2
Bolton Wanderers	0-0	1-2	2-1	■	1-5	0-2	0-3	3-1	2-3	0-5	0-2	1-2	2-1	5-0	0-2	1-1	1-4	2-2	1-2	1-1
Chelsea	3-5	1-3	2-1	3-0	■	3-1	1-1	1-2	2-1	3-3	0-2	3-1	6-1	1-0	1-0	4-1	0-0	2-1	2-1	3-0
Everton	0-1	2-2	1-1	1-2	2-0	■	4-0	0-2	1-0	0-1	3-1	1-1	0-1	0-1	4-0	1-0	1-0	2-0	3-1	2-1
Fulham	2-1	0-0	1-1	2-0	1-1	1-3	■	1-0	2-2	0-5	5-2	2-1	6-0	2-1	2-1	0-3	1-3	1-1	2-1	5-0
Liverpool	1-2	1-1	1-1	3-1	4-1	3-0	0-1	■	1-1	1-1	3-1	1-1	1-0	0-0	1-1	0-0	0-0	0-1	1-2	2-1
Manchester City	1-0	4-1	3-0	2-0	2-1	2-0	3-0	3-0	■	1-0	3-1	5-1	3-2	3-0	3-3	4-0	3-2	4-0	3-0	3-1
Manchester United	8-2	4-0	2-3	3-0	3-1	4-4	1-0	2-1	1-6	■	1-1	2-0	2-0	2-0	1-0	2-0	3-0	2-0	5-0	4-1
Newcastle United	0-0	2-1	3-1	2-0	0-3	2-1	2-1	2-0	0-2	3-0	■	1-0	1-0	3-0	1-1	0-0	2-2	2-3	1-0	2-2
Norwich City	1-2	2-0	3-3	2-0	0-0	2-2	1-1	0-3	1-6	1-2	4-2	■	2-1	1-1	2-1	3-1	0-2	0-1	1-1	2-1
Queens Park Rangers	2-1	1-1	1-1	0-4	1-0	1-1	0-1	3-2	2-3	0-2	0-0	1-2	■	1-0	2-3	3-0	1-0	1-1	3-1	1-2
Stoke City	1-1	0-0	3-1	2-2	0-0	1-1	2-0	1-0	1-1	1-1	1-3	1-0	2-3	■	0-1	2-0	2-1	1-2	2-2	2-1
Sunderland	1-2	2-2	2-1	2-2	1-2	1-1	0-0	1-0	1-0	0-1	0-1	3-0	3-1	4-0	■	2-0	0-0	2-2	1-2	0-0
Swansea City	3-2	0-0	3-0	3-1	1-1	0-2	2-0	1-0	1-0	0-1	0-2	2-3	1-1	2-0	0-0	■	1-1	3-0	0-0	4-4
Tottenham Hotspur	2-1	2-0	2-0	3-0	1-1	2-0	2-0	4-0	1-5	1-3	5-0	1-2	3-1	1-1	1-0	3-1	■	1-0	3-1	1-1
West Bromwich Albion	2-3	0-0	3-0	2-1	1-0	0-1	0-0	0-2	0-0	1-2	1-3	1-2	1-0	0-1	4-0	1-2	1-3	■	1-2	2-0
Wigan Athletic	0-4	0-0	3-3	1-3	1-1	1-1	0-2	0-0	0-1	1-0	4-0	1-1	2-0	2-0	1-4	0-2	1-2	1-1	■	3-2
Wolverhampton Wanderers	0-3	2-3	0-2	2-3	1-2	0-0	2-0	0-3	0-2	0-5	1-2	2-2	0-3	1-2	2-1	2-2	0-2	1-5	3-1	■

Football League Championship 2011/2012 Season	Barnsley	Birmingham City	Blackpool	Brighton & Hove Albion	Bristol City	Burnley	Cardiff City	Coventry City	Crystal Palace	Derby County	Doncaster Rovers	Hull City	Ipswich Town	Leeds United	Leicester City	Middlesbrough	Millwall	Nottingham Forest	Peterborough United	Portsmouth	Reading	Southampton	Watford
Barnsley		1-3	1-3	0-0	1-2	2-0	0-1	2-0	2-1	3-2	2-0	2-1	3-5	4-1	1-1	1-3	1-3	1-1	1-0	2-0	0-4	0-1	1-1
Birmingham City	1-1		3-0	0-0	2-2	2-1	1-1	1-0	3-1	2-2	2-1	0-0	2-1	1-0	2-0	3-0	3-0	1-2	1-1	1-0	2-0	0-0	3-0
Blackpool	1-1	2-2		3-1	5-0	4-0	1-1	2-1	2-1	0-1	2-1	1-1	2-0	1-0	3-3	3-0	1-0	1-2	2-1	1-1	1-0	3-0	0-0
Brighton & Hove Albion	2-0	1-1	2-2		2-0	0-1	2-2	2-1	1-3	2-0	2-1	0-0	3-0	3-3	1-0	1-1	2-2	1-0	2-0	2-0	0-1	3-0	2-2
Bristol City	2-0	0-2	1-3	0-1		3-1	1-2	3-1	2-2	1-1	2-1	1-1	0-3	0-3	3-2	0-1	1-0	0-0	1-2	0-0	2-3	2-0	0-2
Burnley	2-0	1-3	3-1	1-0	1-1		1-1	1-1	1-1	0-0	3-0	1-0	4-0	1-2	1-3	0-2	1-3	5-1	1-1	0-1	0-1	1-1	2-2
Cardiff City	5-3	1-0	1-3	1-3	3-1	0-0		2-2	2-0	2-0	2-0	0-3	2-2	1-1	0-0	2-3	0-0	1-0	3-1	3-2	3-1	2-1	1-1
Coventry City	1-0	1-1	2-2	2-0	1-0	1-2	1-1		1-1	2-0	0-2	0-1	2-3	2-1	0-1	3-1	0-1	1-0	2-2	2-0	1-1	2-4	0-0
Crystal Palace	1-0	1-0	1-1	1-1	1-0	2-0	1-2	2-1		1-1	1-1	0-0	1-1	1-1	1-2	0-1	0-0	3-0	1-0	0-0	0-0	0-2	4-0
Derby County	1-1	2-1	2-1	0-1	2-1	1-2	0-3	1-0	3-2		3-0	0-2	0-0	1-0	0-1	0-1	3-0	1-0	1-1	3-1	0-1	1-1	1-2
Doncaster Rovers	2-0	1-3	1-3	1-1	1-1	1-2	0-0	1-1	1-0	1-2		1-1	2-3	0-3	2-1	1-3	0-3	0-1	1-1	3-4	1-1	1-0	0-0
Hull City	3-1	2-1	0-1	0-0	3-0	2-3	2-1	0-2	0-1	0-1	0-0		2-2	0-0	2-1	2-1	2-0	2-1	1-0	1-0	1-0	0-2	3-2
Ipswich Town	1-0	1-1	2-2	3-1	3-0	1-0	3-0	3-0	0-1	1-0	2-3	0-1		2-1	1-2	1-1	0-3	1-3	3-2	1-0	2-3	2-5	1-2
Leeds United	1-2	1-4	0-5	1-2	2-1	2-1	1-1	1-1	3-2	0-2	3-2	4-1	3-1		1-2	0-1	2-0	3-7	4-1	1-0	0-1	0-1	0-2
Leicester City	1-2	3-1	2-0	1-0	1-2	0-0	2-1	2-0	3-0	4-0	3-0	2-1	1-1	0-1		2-2	0-3	0-0	1-1	1-1	0-2	3-2	2-0
Middlesbrough	2-0	3-1	2-2	1-1	0-2	0-2	1-1	0-0	2-0	0-0	1-0	0-0	0-2	0-0	0-2		1-1	2-1	1-1	2-2	0-2	2-1	1-0
Millwall	0-0	0-6	2-2	1-1	1-2	0-1	0-0	3-0	0-1	0-0	3-2	2-0	4-1	0-1	2-1	1-3		2-0	2-2	1-0	1-2	2-3	0-2
Nottingham Forest	0-0	1-3	0-0	1-1	0-1	0-2	0-1	2-0	0-1	1-2	1-2	0-1	3-2	0-4	2-2	2-0	3-1		0-1	2-0	1-0	0-3	1-1
Peterborough United	3-4	1-1	3-1	1-2	3-0	2-1	4-3	1-0	2-1	3-2	1-2	0-1	7-1	2-3	1-0	1-1	0-3	0-1		0-3	3-1	1-3	2-2
Portsmouth	2-0	4-1	1-0	0-1	0-0	1-5	1-1	2-1	2-1	1-2	3-1	2-0	0-1	0-0	1-1	1-3	0-1	3-0	2-3		1-0	1-1	2-0
Reading	1-2	1-0	3-1	3-0	1-0	1-0	1-2	2-0	2-2	2-2	2-0	0-1	1-0	2-0	3-1	0-0	2-2	1-0	3-2	1-0		1-1	0-2
Southampton	2-0	4-1	2-2	3-0	0-1	2-0	1-1	4-0	2-0	4-0	2-0	2-1	1-1	3-1	0-2	3-0	1-0	3-2	2-1	2-2	1-3		4-0
Watford	2-1	2-2	0-2	1-0	2-2	3-2	1-1	0-0	0-2	0-1	4-1	1-1	2-1	1-1	3-2	2-1	2-1	0-1	3-2	2-0	1-2	0-3	
West Ham United	1-0	3-3	4-0	6-0	0-0	1-2	0-1	1-0	0-0	3-1	1-1	2-1	0-1	2-2	3-2	1-1	2-1	2-1	1-0	4-3	2-4	1-1	1-1

Football League League One 2011/2012 Season	Bournemouth	Brentford	Bury	Carlisle United	Charlton Athletic	Chesterfield	Colchester United	Exeter City	Hartlepool United	Huddersfield Town	Leyton Orient	Milton Keynes Dons	Notts County	Oldham Athletic	Preston North End	Rochdale	Scunthorpe United	Sheffield United	Sheffield Wednesday	Stevenage	Tranmere Rovers	Walsall	Wycombe Wanderers	Yeovil Town
Bournemouth		1-0	1-2	1-1	0-1	0-3	1-1	2-0	1-2	2-0	1-2	0-1	2-1	0-0	1-0	1-1	2-0	0-2	2-0	1-3	2-1	0-2	2-0	0-0
Brentford	1-1		3-0	4-0	0-1	2-1	1-1	2-0	2-1	0-4	5-0	3-3	0-0	2-0	1-3	2-0	0-0	0-2	1-2	0-1	0-2	0-0	5-2	2-0
Bury	1-0	1-1		0-2	1-2	1-1	4-1	2-0	1-2	3-3	1-1	0-0	2-2	0-0	1-0	2-4	0-0	0-3	2-1	1-2	2-0	2-1	1-4	3-2
Carlisle United	2-1	2-2	4-1		0-1	2-1	1-0	4-1	1-2	2-1	4-1	1-3	0-3	3-3	0-0	2-1	0-0	3-2	3-2	1-0	0-0	1-1	2-2	3-2
Charlton Athletic	3-0	2-0	1-1	4-0		3-1	0-2	2-0	3-2	2-0	2-0	2-1	2-4	1-1	5-2	1-1	2-2	1-0	1-1	2-0	1-1	1-0	2-1	3-0
Chesterfield	1-0	1-3	1-0	4-1	0-4		0-1	0-2	2-3	0-2	0-0	1-1	1-3	1-1	0-2	2-1	1-4	0-1	1-0	1-1	1-0	1-1	4-0	2-2
Colchester United	1-1	2-1	4-1	1-1	0-2	1-2		2-0	1-1	1-1	1-1	1-5	4-2	4-1	3-0	0-0	1-1	1-1	1-1	1-6	4-2	1-0	1-1	1-1
Exeter City	0-2	1-2	3-2	0-0	0-1	2-1	1-1		0-0	0-4	3-0	0-2	1-1	2-0	1-2	3-1	0-0	2-2	2-1	1-1	3-0	4-2	1-3	1-1
Hartlepool United	0-0	0-0	3-0	4-0	0-4	1-2	0-1	2-0		0-0	2-1	1-1	3-0	0-1	0-1	1-1	0-1	0-0	0-2	1-1	1-3	0-1		
Huddersfield Town	0-1	3-2	1-1	1-1	1-0	1-0	3-2	2-0	1-0		2-2	1-1	2-1	1-0	3-1	2-2	1-0	0-2	2-1	2-0	1-1	3-0	2-0	
Leyton Orient	1-3	2-0	1-0	1-2	1-0	1-1	0-1	3-0	1-1	1-3		0-3	0-3	1-3	2-1	2-1	1-3	1-1	0-1	0-0	0-1	1-1	1-3	2-2
Milton Keynes Dons	2-2	1-2	2-1	1-2	1-1	6-2	1-0	3-0	2-2	1-1	4-1		3-0	5-0	0-1	3-1	0-0	1-0	1-1	1-0	3-0	0-1	4-3	0-1
Notts County	3-1	1-1	2-4	2-0	1-2	1-0	4-1	2-1	3-0	2-2	1-2	1-1		1-0	0-0	2-3	2-5	1-2	1-0	3-2	2-1	1-1	3-1	
Oldham Athletic	1-0	0-2	0-2	2-1	0-1	5-2	1-1	0-0	0-1	1-1	0-1	2-1	3-2		1-1	2-0	1-2	0-2	0-2	1-1	1-1	2-0	1-2	
Preston North End	1-3	1-3	1-1	3-3	2-2	0-0	2-4	1-0	1-0	1-0	0-2	1-1	2-0	3-3		0-1	0-0	2-4	0-2	0-0	2-1	0-0	3-2	4-3
Rochdale	1-0	1-2	3-0	0-0	2-3	1-1	2-2	3-2	1-3	2-2	0-2	1-2	0-1	3-2	1-1		1-0	2-5	0-0	1-5	0-2	3-3	2-1	0-0
Scunthorpe United	1-1	0-0	1-3	1-2	1-1	2-2	1-1	1-0	0-2	2-2	2-3	0-3	0-0	1-2	1-1	1-0		1-1	1-3	1-1	4-2	0-1	4-1	2-1
Sheffield United	2-1	2-0	4-0	1-0	0-2	4-1	3-0	4-4	3-1	0-3	3-1	2-1	2-1	2-3	2-1	3-0	2-1		2-2	2-2	1-1	3-2	3-0	4-0
Sheffield Wednesday	3-0	0-0	4-1	2-1	0-1	3-1	2-0	3-0	2-2	4-4	1-0	3-1	2-1	3-0	2-0	2-0	3-2	1-0		0-1	2-1	2-2	2-0	2-1
Stevenage	2-2	2-1	3-0	1-0	1-0	2-2	0-0	0-0	2-2	2-2	0-1	4-2	0-2	1-0	1-1	4-2	1-2	2-1	5-1		2-1	0-0	1-1	0-0
Tranmere Rovers	0-0	2-2	2-0	1-2	1-1	1-0	0-0	2-0	1-1	1-1	2-0	0-2	1-1	2-1	0-0	1-1	1-1	1-2	3-0	2-1		2-0	0-0	
Walsall	2-2	0-1	2-4	1-1	1-1	3-2	3-1	1-2	0-0	1-1	1-0	0-2	0-1	0-1	1-0	0-0	2-2	3-2	2-1	1-1	0-1		2-0	1-1
Wycombe Wanderers	0-1	0-1	0-2	1-1	1-2	3-2	0-0	3-1	5-0	0-6	4-2	1-1	3-4	2-2	3-4	3-0	1-1	1-0	1-2	0-1	2-1	1-1		2-3
Yeovil Town	1-3	2-1	1-3	0-3	2-3	3-2	3-2	2-2	0-1	0-1	2-2	0-1	1-0	3-1	2-1	3-1	2-2	0-1	2-3	0-6	2-1	2-1	1-0	

Football League League Two 2011/2012 Season	Accrington Stanley	AFC Wimbledon	Aldershot Town	Barnet	Bradford City	Bristol Rovers	Burton Albion	Cheltenham Town	Crawley Town	Crewe Alexandra	Dagenham & Redbridge	Gillingham	Hereford United	Macclesfield Town	Morecambe	Northamtpon Town	Oxford United	Plymouth Argyle	Port Vale	Rotherham United	Shrewsbury Town	Southend United	Swindon Town	Torquay United
Accrington Stanley	■	2-1	3-2	0-3	1-0	2-1	2-1	0-1	0-1	0-2	3-0	4-3	2-1	4-0	1-1	2-1	0-2	0-4	2-2	1-1	1-1	1-2	0-2	3-1
AFC Wimbledon	0-2	■	1-2	1-1	3-1	2-3	4-0	4-1	2-5	1-3	2-1	3-1	1-1	2-1	1-1	0-3	0-2	1-2	3-2	1-2	3-1	1-4	1-1	2-0
Aldershot Town	0-0	1-1	■	4-1	1-0	1-0	2-0	1-0	0-1	3-1	1-1	1-2	1-0	1-2	1-0	0-1	0-3	0-0	1-2	2-2	1-0	2-0	2-1	0-1
Barnet	0-0	4-0	2-1	■	0-4	2-0	3-6	2-2	1-2	2-0	2-2	2-2	1-1	2-1	0-2	1-2	0-2	2-0	1-3	1-1	1-2	0-3	0-2	0-1
Bradford City	1-1	1-2	1-2	4-2	■	2-2	1-1	0-1	1-2	3-0	0-1	2-2	1-1	1-0	2-2	2-1	2-1	1-1	1-1	2-3	3-1	2-0	0-0	1-0
Bristol Rovers	5-1	1-0	0-1	0-2	2-1	■	7-1	1-3	0-0	2-5	2-0	2-2	0-0	0-0	2-1	2-1	0-0	2-3	0-3	5-2	1-0	1-0	1-1	1-2
Burton Albion	0-2	3-2	0-4	1-2	2-2	2-1	■	0-2	0-0	1-0	1-1	1-0	0-2	1-0	3-2	0-1	1-1	2-1	1-1	1-1	1-1	0-2	2-0	1-4
Cheltenham Town	4-1	0-0	2-0	2-0	3-1	0-2	2-0	■	3-1	0-1	2-1	0-3	0-0	2-0	1-2	2-2	0-2	1-0	2-0	1-0	0-0	3-0	1-0	0-1
Crawley Town	1-1	1-1	2-2	1-0	3-1	4-1	3-0	4-2	■	1-1	3-1	1-2	0-3	2-0	1-1	3-1	4-1	2-0	3-2	3-0	2-1	3-0	0-3	0-1
Crewe Alexandra	2-0	3-3	2-2	3-1	1-0	3-0	3-2	1-0	1-1	■	4-1	1-2	1-0	0-1	0-1	1-1	3-1	3-2	1-1	1-2	1-1	1-3	2-0	0-3
Dagenham & Redbridge	2-1	0-2	2-5	3-0	1-0	4-0	1-1	0-5	1-1	2-1	■	2-1	0-1	2-0	1-2	0-1	0-1	2-3	1-2	3-2	0-2	2-3	1-0	1-
Gillingham	1-1	3-4	1-0	3-1	0-0	4-1	3-1	1-0	0-1	3-4	1-2	■	5-4	2-0	2-0	4-3	1-0	3-0	1-1	0-0	0-1	1-2	3-1	2-
Hereford United	1-1	2-1	0-2	1-0	2-0	1-2	2-3	1-1	1-1	0-1	1-0	1-6	■	0-4	0-3	0-0	0-1	1-1	1-2	2-3	0-2	2-3	1-2	3-
Macclesfield Town	1-1	4-0	0-1	0-0	1-0	0-0	0-2	1-3	2-2	2-2	0-1	0-0	2-2	■	1-1	3-1	1-1	1-1	2-1	0-0	1-3	0-2	2-0	1-
Morecambe	1-2	1-2	2-0	0-1	1-1	2-3	2-2	3-1	6-0	1-2	1-2	2-1	0-1	1-0	■	1-2	0-0	2-2	0-0	3-3	0-1	1-0	0-1	1-
Northampton Town	0-0	1-0	3-1	1-2	1-3	3-2	2-3	2-3	0-1	1-1	2-1	1-1	1-3	3-2	0-2	■	2-1	0-0	1-2	1-1	2-7	2-5	1-2	0-
Oxford United	1-1	1-0	1-1	2-1	1-1	3-0	2-2	1-3	1-1	0-1	2-1	0-0	2-2	1-1	1-2	2-0	■	5-1	2-1	2-1	2-0	0-2	2-0	2-
Plymouth Argyle	2-2	0-2	1-0	0-0	1-0	1-1	2-1	1-2	1-1	0-1	0-0	0-1	1-1	2-0	1-1	4-1	1-1	■	0-2	1-4	1-0	2-2	0-1	1-
Port Vale	4-1	1-2	4-0	1-2	3-2	1-0	3-0	1-2	2-2	1-1	0-1	2-1	1-0	1-0	0-4	3-0	3-0	1-0	■	2-0	2-3	2-3	0-2	0-
Rotherham United	1-0	1-0	2-0	2-2	3-0	0-1	0-1	1-0	1-2	1-1	3-1	3-0	1-0	4-2	3-2	1-0	1-0	1-0	0-1	■	1-1	0-4	1-2	0-
Shrewsbury Town	1-0	0-0	1-1	3-2	1-0	1-0	1-0	2-0	2-1	2-0	1-0	2-0	3-1	1-0	2-0	1-1	2-2	1-1	1-0	3-1	■	2-1	2-1	2
Southend United	2-2	2-0	0-1	3-0	0-1	1-1	0-1	4-0	0-0	1-0	1-1	1-0	1-0	2-0	1-1	2-2	2-1	2-0	3-0	0-2	3-0	■	1-4	4
Swindon Town	2-0	2-0	2-0	4-0	0-0	0-0	2-0	1-0	3-0	3-0	4-0	2-0	3-3	1-0	3-0	1-0	1-2	1-0	5-0	3-2	2-1	2-0	■	2
Torquay United	1-0	4-0	1-0	1-0	1-2	2-2	2-2	2-2	1-3	1-1	1-0	2-5	2-0	3-0	1-1	1-0	0-0	3-1	2-1	3-3	1-0	0-0	1-0	■

F.A. Premier League

Season 2011/2012

Manchester City	38	28	5	5	93	29	89
Manchester United	38	28	5	5	89	33	89
Arsenal	38	21	7	10	74	49	70
Tottenham Hotspur	38	20	9	9	66	41	69
Newcastle United	38	19	8	11	56	51	65
Chelsea	38	18	10	10	65	46	64
Everton	38	15	11	12	50	40	56
Liverpool	38	14	10	14	47	40	52
Fulham	38	14	10	14	48	51	52
West Bromwich Albion	38	13	8	17	45	52	47
Swansea City	38	12	11	15	44	51	47
Norwich City	38	12	11	15	52	66	47
Sunderland	38	11	12	15	45	46	45
Stoke City	38	11	12	15	36	53	45
Wigan Athletic	38	11	10	17	42	62	43
Aston Villa	38	7	17	14	37	53	38
Queens Park Rangers	38	10	7	21	43	66	37
Bolton Wanderers	38	10	6	22	46	77	36
Blackburn Rovers	38	8	7	23	48	78	31
Wolverhampton Wanderers	38	5	10	23	40	82	25

Champions: Manchester City

Relegated: Bolton Wanderers, Blackburn Rovers and Wolverhampton Wanderers

Football League – The Championship

Season 2011/2012

Reading	46	27	8	11	69	41	89
Southampton	46	26	10	10	85	46	88
West Ham United	46	24	14	8	81	48	86
Birmingham City	46	20	16	10	78	51	76
Blackpool	46	20	15	11	79	59	75
Cardiff City	46	19	18	9	66	53	75
Middlesbrough	46	18	16	12	52	51	70
Hull City	46	19	11	16	47	44	68
Leicester City	46	18	12	16	66	55	66
Brighton & Hove Albion	46	17	15	14	52	52	66
Watford	46	16	16	14	56	64	64
Derby County	46	18	10	18	50	58	64
Burnley	46	17	11	18	61	58	62
Leeds United	46	17	10	19	65	68	61
Ipswich Town	46	17	10	19	69	77	61
Millwall	46	15	12	19	55	57	57
Crystal Palace	46	13	17	16	46	51	56
Peterborough United	46	13	11	22	67	77	50
Nottingham Forest	46	14	8	24	48	63	50
Bristol City	46	12	13	21	44	68	49
Barnsley	46	13	9	24	49	74	48
Portsmouth	46	13	11	22	50	59	40
Coventry City	46	9	13	24	41	65	40
Doncaster Rovers	46	8	12	26	43	80	36

Portsmouth had 10 points deducted

Promotion Play-offs

Cardiff City 0   West Ham United 2
Blackpool 1   Birmingham City 0

West Ham United 3   Cardiff City 0
West Ham United won 5-0 on aggregate
Birmingham City 2   Blackpool 2
Blackpool won 3-2 on aggregate

Blackpool 1   West Ham United 2

Promoted: Reading, Southampton and West Ham United

Relegated: Portsmouth, Coventry City and Doncaster Rovers

Football League – League One

Season 2011/2012

Charlton Athletic	46	30	11	5	82	36	101
Sheffield Wednesday	46	28	9	9	81	48	93
Sheffield United	46	27	9	10	92	51	90
Huddersfield Town	46	21	18	7	79	47	81
Milton Keynes Dons	46	22	14	10	84	47	80
Stevenage	46	21	10	15	69	44	73
Notts County	46	18	19	9	75	63	73
Carlisle United	46	18	15	13	65	66	69
Brentford	46	18	13	15	63	52	67
Colchester United	46	13	20	13	61	66	59
Bournemouth	46	15	13	18	48	52	58
Tranmere Rovers	46	14	14	18	49	53	56
Hartlepool United	46	14	14	18	50	55	56
Bury	46	15	11	20	60	79	56
Preston North End	46	13	15	18	54	68	54
Oldham Athletic	46	14	12	20	50	66	54
Yeovil Town	46	14	12	20	59	80	54
Scunthorpe United	46	10	22	14	55	59	52
Walsall	46	10	20	16	51	57	50
Leyton Orient	46	13	11	22	48	75	50
Wycombe Wanderers	46	11	10	25	65	88	43
Chesterfield	46	10	12	24	55	81	42
Exeter City	46	10	12	24	46	75	42
Rochdale	46	8	14	24	47	81	38

Football League – League Two

Season 2011/2012

Swindon Town	46	29	6	11	75	32	
Shrewsbury Town	46	26	10	10	66	41	
Crawley Town	46	23	15	8	76	54	
Southend United	46	25	8	13	77	48	
Torquay United	46	23	12	11	63	50	
Cheltenham Town	46	23	8	15	66	50	
Crewe Alexandra	46	20	12	14	67	59	
Gillingham	46	20	10	16	79	62	
Oxford United	46	17	17	12	59	48	
Rotherham United	46	18	13	15	67	63	
Aldershot Town	46	19	9	18	54	52	
Port Vale	46	20	9	17	68	60	
Bristol Rovers	46	15	12	19	60	70	
Accrington Stanley	46	14	15	17	54	66	
Morecambe	46	14	14	18	63	57	
AFC Wimbledon	46	15	9	22	62	78	
Burton Albion	46	14	12	20	54	81	
Bradford City	46	12	14	20	54	59	
Dagenham & Redbridge	46	14	8	24	50	72	
Northampton Town	46	12	11	23	56	79	
Plymouth Argyle	46	10	16	20	47	64	
Barnet	46	12	10	24	52	79	
Hereford United	46	10	14	22	50	70	
Macclesfield Town	46	8	13	25	39	64	

Port Vale had 10 points deducted

Promotion Play-offs

Stevenage 0   Sheffield United 0
Milton Keynes Dons 0   Huddersfield Town 2

Sheffield United 1   Stevenage 0
Sheffield United won 1-0 on aggregate
Huddersfield Town 1   Milton Keynes Dons 2
Huddersfield Town won 3-2 on aggregate

Huddersfield Town 0   Sheffield United .... 0 (aet.)
Huddersfield Town won 8-7 on penalties

Promoted: Charlton Athletic, Sheffield Wednesday and Huddersfield Town

Relegated: Wycombe Wanderers, Chesterfield, Exeter City and Rochdale

Promotion Play-offs

Crewe Alexandra 1   Southend United ....
Cheltenham Town 2   Torquay United ....

Southend United 2   Crewe Alexandra ....
Crewe Alexandra won 3-2 on aggregate
Torquay United 1   Cheltenham Town ....
Cheltenham Town won 4-1 on aggregate

Cheltenham Town 0   Crewe Alexandra ....

Promoted: Swindon Town, Shrewsbury Town, Crawley Town and Crewe Alexandra

Relegated: Hereford United and Macclesfield Town

F.A. Cup 2011/2012

Round 1	AFC Totton	8	Bradford Park Avenue	1	
Round 1	AFC Wimbledon	0	Scunthorpe United	0	
Round 1	Alfreton Town	0	Carlisle United	4	
Round 1	Barrow	1	Rotherham United	2	
Round 1	Blyth Spartans	0	Gateshead	2	
Round 1	Bournemouth	3	Gillingham	3	
Round 1	Bradford City	1	Rochdale	0	
Round 1	Brentford	1	Basingstoke Town	0	
Round 1	Bristol Rovers	3	Corby Town	1	
Round 1	Bury	0	Crawley Town	2	
Round 1	Cambridge United	2	Wrexham	2	
Round 1	Chelmsford City	4	AFC Telford United	0	
Round 1	Chesterfield	1	Torquay United	3	
Round 1	Crewe Alexandra	1	Colchester United	4	
Round 1	Dagenham & Redbridge	1	Bath City	1	
Round 1	East Thurrock United	0	Macclesfield Town	3	
Round 1	Exeter City	1	Walsall	1	
Round 1	FC Halifax Town	0	Charlton Athletic	4	
Round 1	Fleetwood Town	2	Wycombe Wanderers	0	
Round 1	Hartlepool United	0	Stevenage	1	
Round 1	Hereford United	0	Yeovil Town	3	
Round 1	Hinckley United	2	Tamworth	2	
Round 1	Leyton Orient	3	Bromley	0	
Round 1	Luton Town	1	Northampton Town	0	
Round 1	Maidenhead United	1	Aldershot Town	1	
Round 1	Milton Keynes Dons	6	Nantwich Town	0	
Round 1	Morecambe	1	Sheffield Wednesday	2	
Round 1	Newport County	0	Shrewsbury Town	1	
Round 1	Notts County	4	Accrington Stanley	1	
Round 1	Oldham Athletic	3	Burton Albion	1	
Round 1	Plymouth Argyle	3	Stourbridge	3	
Round 1	Port Vale	0	Grimsby Town	0	
Round 1	Preston North End	0	Southend United	0	
Round 1	Redbridge	0	Oxford City	0	
Round 1	Salisbury City	3	Arlesey Town	1	
Round 1	Sheffield United	3	Oxford United	0	
Round 1	Southport	1	Barnet	2	
Round 1	Sutton United	1	Kettering Town	0	
Round 1	Swindon Town	4	Huddersfield Town	1	
Round 1	Tranmere Rovers	0	Cheltenham Town	1	
Replay	Aldershot Town	2	Maidenhead United	0	
Replay	Bath City	1	Dagenham & Redbridge	3	(aet)
Replay	Gillingham	3	Bournemouth	2	
Replay	Grimsby Town	1	Port Vale	0	
Replay	Oxford City	1	Redbridge	2	(aet)
Replay	Scunthorpe United	0	AFC Wimbledon	1	
Replay	Southend United	1	Preston North End	0	
Replay	Stourbridge	2	Plymouth Argyle	0	
Replay	Tamworth	1	Hinckley United	0	
Replay	Walsall	3	Exeter City	2	(aet)
Replay	Wrexham	2	Cambridge United	1	
Round 2	AFC Totton	1	Bristol Rovers	6	
Round 2	Barnet	1	Milton Keynes Dons	3	

Round 2	Bradford City	3	AFC Wimbledon	1	
Round 2	Brentford	0	Wrexham	1	
Round 2	Charlton Athletic	2	Carlisle United	0	
Round 2	Chelmsford City	1	Macclesfield Town	1	
Round 2	Colchester United	0	Swindon Town	1	
Round 2	Crawley Town	5	Redbridge	0	
Round 2	Dagenham & Redbridge	1	Walsall	1	
Round 2	Fleetwood Town	2	Yeovil Town	2	
Round 2	Gateshead	1	Tamworth	2	
Round 2	Leyton Orient	0	Gillingham	1	
Round 2	Luton Town	2	Cheltenham Town	4	
Round 2	Salisbury City	0	Grimsby Town	0	
Round 2	Sheffield United	3	Torquay United	2	
Round 2	Sheffield Wednesday	1	Aldershot Town	0	
Round 2	Shrewsbury Town	2	Rotherham United	1	
Round 2	Southend United	1	Oldham Athletic	1	
Round 2	Stourbridge	0	Stevenage	3	
Round 2	Sutton United	0	Notts County	2	
Replay	Grimsby Town	2	Salisbury City	3	(aet)
Replay	Macclesfield Town	1	Chelmsford City	0	
Replay	Oldham Athletic	1	Southend United	0	
Replay	Walsall	0	Dagenham & Redbridge	0	(aet)
	Dagenham & Redbridge won 3-2 on penalties				
Replay	Yeovil Town	0	Fleetwood Town	2	
Round 3	Arsenal	1	Leeds United	0	
Round 3	Barnsley	2	Swansea City	4	
Round 3	Birmingham City	0	Wolverhampton Wanderers	0	
Round 3	Brighton & Hove Albion	1	Wrexham	1	
Round 3	Bristol Rovers	1	Aston Villa	3	
Round 3	Chelsea	4	Portsmouth	0	
Round 3	Coventry City	1	Southampton	2	
Round 3	Crawley Town	1	Bristol City	0	
Round 3	Dagenham & Redbridge	0	Millwall	0	
Round 3	Derby County	1	Crystal Palace	0	
Round 3	Doncaster Rovers	0	Notts County	2	
Round 3	Everton	2	Tamworth	0	
Round 3	Fleetwood Town	1	Blackpool	5	
Round 3	Fulham	4	Charlton Athletic	0	
Round 3	Gillingham	1	Stoke City	3	
Round 3	Hull City	3	Ipswich Town	1	
Round 3	Liverpool	5	Oldham Athletic	1	
Round 3	Macclesfield Town	2	Bolton Wanderers	2	
Round 3	Manchester City	2	Manchester United	3	
Round 3	Middlesbrough	1	Shrewsbury Town	0	
Round 3	Milton Keynes Dons	1	Queen's Park Rangers	1	
Round 3	Newcastle United	2	Blackburn Rovers	1	
Round 3	Norwich City	4	Burnley	1	
Round 3	Nottingham Forest	0	Leicester City	0	
Round 3	Peterborough United	0	Sunderland	2	
Round 3	Reading	0	Stevenage	1	
Round 3	Sheffield United	3	Salisbury City	1	
Round 3	Sheffield Wednesday	1	West Ham United	0	
Round 3	Swindon Town	2	Wigan Athletic	1	
Round 3	Tottenham Hotspur	3	Cheltenham Town	0	
Round 3	Watford	4	Bradford City	2	
Round 3	West Bromwich Albion	4	Cardiff City	2	

Replay	Bolton Wanderers	2	Macclesfield Town	0	
Replay	Leicester City	4	Nottingham Forest	0	
Replay	Millwall	5	Dagenham & Redbridge	0	
Replay	Queen's Park Rangers	1	Milton Keynes Dons	0	
Replay	Wolverhampton Wanderers	0	Birmingham City	1	
Replay	Wrexham	1	Brighton & Hove Albion	1	(aet)
	Brighton & Hove Albion won 5-4 on penalties				
Round 4	Arsenal	3	Aston Villa	2	
Round 4	Blackpool	1	Sheffield Wednesday	1	
Round 4	Bolton Wanderers	2	Swansea City	1	
Round 4	Brighton & Hove Albion	1	Newcastle United	0	
Round 4	Derby County	0	Stoke City	2	
Round 4	Everton	2	Fulham	1	
Round 4	Hull City	0	Crawley Town	1	
Round 4	Leicester City	2	Swindon Town	0	
Round 4	Liverpool	2	Manchester United	1	
Round 4	Millwall	1	Southampton	1	
Round 4	Queen's Park Rangers	0	Chelsea	1	
Round 4	Sheffield United	0	Birmingham City	4	
Round 4	Stevenage	1	Notts County	0	
Round 4	Sunderland	1	Middlesbrough	1	
Round 4	Watford	0	Tottenham Hotspur	1	
Round 4	West Bromwich Albion	1	Norwich City	2	
Replay	Middlesbrough	1	Sunderland	2	(aet)
Replay	Sheffield Wednesday	0	Blackpool	3	
Replay	Southampton	2	Millwall	3	
Round 5	Chelsea	1	Birmingham City	1	
Round 5	Crawley Town	0	Stoke City	2	
Round 5	Everton	2	Blackpool	0	
Round 5	Liverpool	6	Brighton & Hove Albion	1	
Round 5	Millwall	0	Bolton Wanderers	2	
Round 5	Norwich City	1	Leicester City	2	
Round 5	Stevenage	0	Tottenham Hotspur	0	
Round 5	Sunderland	2	Arsenal	0	
Replay	Birmingham City	0	Chelsea	2	
Replay	Tottenham Hotspur	3	Stevenage	1	
Round 6	Chelsea	5	Leicester City	2	
Round 6	Everton	1	Sunderland	1	
Round 6	Liverpool	2	Stoke City	1	
Round 6	Tottenham Hotspur	3	Bolton Wanderers	1	
Replay	Sunderland	0	Everton	2	
Semi-final	Chelsea	5	Tottenham Hotspur	1	
Semi-final	Liverpool	2	Everton	1	
FINAL	Chelsea	2	Liverpool	1	

Football League Cup 2011/2012

Prelim. Round	Crawley Town	3	AFC Wimbledon	2	
Round 1	Accrington Stanley	0	Scunthorpe United	2	
Round 1	Barnsley	0	Morecambe	2	
Round 1	Bournemouth	5	Dagenham & Redbridge	0	
Round 1	Brighton & Hove Albion	1	Gillingham	0	
Round 1	Bristol City	0	Swindon Town	1	
Round 1	Bristol Rovers	1	Watford	1	(aet)
	Bristol Rovers won 4-2 on penalties				
Round 1	Burnley	6	Burton Albion	3	(aet)
Round 1	Bury	3	Coventry City	1	
Round 1	Charlton Athletic	2	Reading	1	
Round 1	Cheltenham Town	1	Milton Keynes Dons	4	
Round 1	Crystal Palace	2	Crawley Town	0	
Round 1	Derby County	2	Shrewsbury Town	3	
Round 1	Doncaster Rovers	3	Tranmere Rovers	0	
Round 1	Exeter City	2	Yeovil Town	0	
Round 1	Hartlepool United	1	Sheffield United	1	(aet)
	Sheffield United won 4-3 on penalties				
Round 1	Hereford United	1	Brentford	0	
Round 1	Hull City	0	Macclesfield Town	2	
Round 1	Ipswich Town	1	Northampton Town	2	
Round 1	Leeds United	3	Bradford City	2	
Round 1	Nottingham Forest	3	Notts County	3	(aet)
	Nottingham Forest won 4-3 on penalties				
Round 1	Oldham Athletic	1	Carlisle United	1	(aet)
	Carlisle United won 4-2 on penalties				
Round 1	Oxford United	1	Cardiff City	3	(aet)
Round 1	Plymouth Argyle	0	Millwall	1	
Round 1	Port Vale	2	Huddersfield Town	4	
Round 1	Portsmouth	0	Barnet	1	
Round 1	Preston North End	3	Crewe Alexandra	2	
Round 1	Rochdale	3	Chesterfield	2	(aet)
Round 1	Rotherham United	1	Leicester City	4	
Round 1	Sheffield Wednesday	0	Blackpool	0	(aet)
	Sheffield Wednesday won 4-2 on penalties				
Round 1	Southampton	4	Torquay United	1	
Round 1	Southend United	1	Leyton Orient	1	(aet)
	Leyton Orient won 4-3 on penalties				
Round 1	Stevenage	3	Peterborough United	4	(aet)
Round 1	Walsall	0	Middlesbrough	3	
Round 1	West Ham United	1	Aldershot Town	2	
Round 1	Wycombe Wanderers	3	Colchester United	3	(aet)
	Wycombe Wanderers won 5-4 on penalties				
Round 2	Aldershot Town	2	Carlisle United	0	
Round 2	Aston Villa	2	Hereford United	0	
Round 2	Blackburn Rovers	3	Sheffield Wednesday	1	
Round 2	Bolton Wanderers	2	Macclesfield Town	1	
Round 2	Bournemouth	1	West Bromwich Albion	4	
Round 2	Brighton & Hove Albion	1	Sunderland	0	(aet)
Round 2	Burnley	3	Barnet	2	(aet)
Round 2	Bury	2	Leicester City	4	
Round 2	Cardiff City	5	Huddersfield Town	3	(aet)
Round 2	Charlton Athletic	0	Preston North End	2	
Round 2	Crystal Palace	2	Wigan Athletic	1	
Round 2	Doncaster Rovers	1	Leeds United	2	

Round 2	Everton	3	Sheffield United	1	
Round 2	Exeter City	1	Liverpool	3	
Round 2	Leyton Orient	3	Bristol Rovers	2	
Round 2	Millwall	2	Morecambe	0	
Round 2	Northampton Town	0	Wolverhampton Wan.	4	
Round 2	Norwich City	0	Milton Keynes Dons	4	
Round 2	Peterborough United	0	Middlesbrough	2	
Round 2	Queen's Park Rangers	0	Rochdale	2	
Round 2	Scunthorpe United	1	Newcastle United	2	(aet)
Round 2	Shrewsbury Town	3	Swansea City	1	
Round 2	Swindon Town	1	Southampton	3	
Round 2	Wycombe Wanderers	1	Nottingham Forest	4	
Round 3	Aldershot Town	2	Rochdale	1	
Round 3	Arsenal	3	Shrewsbury Town	1	
Round 3	Aston Villa	0	Bolton Wanderers	2	
Round 3	Blackburn Rovers	3	Leyton Orient	2	
Round 3	Brighton & Hove Albion	1	Liverpool	2	
Round 3	Burnley	2	Milton Keynes Dons	1	
Round 3	Cardiff City	2	Leicester City	2	(aet)
	Cardiff City won 7-6 on penalties				
Round 3	Chelsea	0	Fulham	0	(aet)
	Chelsea won 4-3 on penalties				
Round 3	Crystal Palace	2	Middlesbrough	1	
Round 3	Everton	2	West Bromwich Albion	1	(aet)
Round 3	Leeds United	0	Manchester United	3	
Round 3	Manchester City	2	Birmingham City	0	
Round 3	Nottingham Forest	3	Newcastle United	4	
Round 3	Southampton	2	Preston North End	1	
Round 3	Stoke City	0	Tottenham Hotspur	0	(aet)
	Stoke City won 7-6 on penalties				
Round 3	Wolverhampton Wanderers	5	Millwall	0	
Round 4	Aldershot Town	0	Manchester United	3	
Round 4	Arsenal	2	Bolton Wanderers	1	
Round 4	Blackburn Rovers	4	Newcastle United	3	(aet)
Round 4	Cardiff City	1	Burnley	0	
Round 4	Crystal Palace	2	Southampton	0	
Round 4	Everton	1	Chelsea	2	(aet)
Round 4	Stoke City	1	Liverpool	2	
Round 4	Wolverhampton Wanderers	2	Manchester City	5	
Round 5	Arsenal	0	Manchester City	1	
Round 5	Cardiff City	2	Blackburn Rovers	0	
Round 5	Chelsea	0	Liverpool	2	
Round 5	Manchester United	1	Crystal Palace	2	(aet)
Semi-Finals					
1st leg	Crystal Palace	1	Cardiff City	0	
2nd leg	Cardiff City	1	Crystal Palace	0	(aet)
	Aggregate 1-1. Cardiff City won 3-1 on penalties				
1st leg	Manchester City	0	Liverpool	1	
2nd leg	Liverpool	2	Manchester City	2	
	Liverpool won 3-2 on aggregate				
FINAL	Liverpool	2	Cardiff City	2	(aet)
	Liverpool won 3-2 on penalties				

ENGLAND INTERNATIONAL LINE-UPS AND STATISTICS 2010-2011

11th August 2010
v HUNGARY   *Wembley*

J. Hart	Manchester City
G. Johnson	Liverpool
A. Cole	Chelsea (sub. K. Gibbs 46)
S. Gerrard	Liverpool (sub. J. Wilshire 82)
P. Jagielka	Everton
J. Terry	Chelsea (sub. M. Dawson 46)
T. Walcott	Arsenal (sub. B. Zamora 46)
F. Lampard	Chelsea (sub. A. Young 46)
A. Johnson	Manchester City
W. Rooney	Manchester Utd. (sub. J. Milner 66)
G. Barry	Manchester City

Result 2-1   Gerrard 2

3rd September 2010
v BULGARIA (ECQ)   *Wembley*

J. Hart	Manchester City
G. Johnson	Liverpool
A. Cole	Chelsea
S. Gerrard	Liverpool
M. Dawson	Tottenham Hotspur (sub. G. Cahill 57)
P. Jagielka	Everton
T. Walcott	Arsenal (sub. A. Johnson 74)
G. Barry	Manchester City
J. Defoe	Tottenham Hotspur (sub. A. Young 87)
W. Rooney	Manchester United
J. Milner	Manchester City

Result 4-0   Defoe 3, Johnson

7th September 2010
v SWITZERLAND (ECQ)   *Basle*

J. Hart	Manchester City
G. Johnson	Liverpool
A. Cole	Chelsea
S. Gerrard	Liverpool
J. Lescott	Manchester City
P. Jagielka	Everton
T. Walcott	Arsenal (sub. A. Johnson 13)
G. Barry	Manchester City
J. Defoe	Tottenham Hotspur (sub. D. Bent 70)
W. Rooney	Man. Utd. (sub. S. Wright-Phillips 79)
J. Milner	Manchester City

Result 3-1   Rooney, Johnson, Bent

12th October 2010
v MONTENEGRO (ECQ)   *Wembley*

J. Hart	Manchester City
G. Johnson	Liverpool
A. Cole	Chelsea
S. Gerrard	Liverpool
R. Ferdinand	Manchester United
J. Lescott	Manchester City
A. Young	Aston Villa (sub. S. Wright-Phillips 74)
G. Barry	Manchester City
P. Crouch	Tottenham Hotspur (sub. K. Davies 69)
W. Rooney	Manchester United
A. Johnson	Manchester City

Result 0-0

17th November 2010
v FRANCE   *Wembley*

B. Foster	Birmingham City
P. Jagielka	Everton
K. Gibbs	Arsenal (sub. S. Warnock 72)
S. Gerrard	Liverpool (sub. P. Crouch 84)
R. Ferdinand	Man. United (sub. M. Richards 46)
J. Lescott	Manchester City
T. Walcott	Arsenal (sub. A. Johnson 46)
J. Henderson	Sunderland
A. Caroll	Newcastle Utd. (sub. J. Bothroyd 72)
G. Barry	Manchester City (sub. A. Young 46)
J. Milner	Manchester City

Result 1-2   Crouch

9th February 2011
v DENMARK   *Copenhagen*

J. Hart	Manchester City
G. Johnson	Liverpool
A. Cole	Chelsea (sub. L. Baines 81)
J. Wilshere	Arsenal (sub. G. Barry 46)
M. Dawson	Tottenham Hotspur (sub. G. Cahill 60)
J. Terry	Chelsea
T. Walcott	Arsenal (sub. S. Downing 67)
F. Lampard	Chelsea (sub. S. Parker 46)
D. Bent	Aston Villa
W. Rooney	Manchester Utd. (sub. A. Young 46)
J. Milner	Manchester City

Result 2-1   Bent, Young

ENGLAND INTERNATIONAL LINE-UPS AND STATISTICS 2011

26th March 2011
v WALES (ECQ)   *Cardiff*

J. Hart	Manchester City
G. Johnson	Liverpool
A. Cole	Chelsea
S. Parker	West Ham Utd. (sub. P. Jagielka 88)
M. Dawson	Tottenham Hotspur
J. Terry	Chelsea
F. Lampard	Chelsea
J. Wilshere	Arsenal (sub. S. Downing 82)
D. Bent	Aston Villa
W. Rooney	Manchester Utd. (sub. J. Milner 70)
A. Young	Aston Villa

Result 2-0   Lampard (pen), Bent

29th March 2011
v GHANA   *Wembley*

J. Hart	Manchester City
G. Johnson	Liverpool (sub. J. Lescott 46)
L. Baines	Everton
G. Barry	Manchester City
G. Cahill	Bolton Wanderers
P. Jagielka	Everton
J. Milner	Manchester City
J. Wilshere	Arsenal (sub. M. Jarvis 69)
A. Caroll	Liverpool (sub. J. Defoe 59)
A. Young	Aston Villa (sub. D. Welbeck 81)
S. Downing	Aston Villa

Result 1-1   Carroll

4th June 2011
v SWITZERLAND (ECQ)   *Wembley*

J. Hart	Manchester City
G. Johnson	Liverpool
A. Cole	Chelsea (sub. L Baines 30)
S. Parker	West Ham United
R. Ferdinand	Manchester United
J. Terry	Chelsea
T. Walcott	Arsenal (sub. S. Downing 77)
F. Lampard	Chelsea (sub. A. Young 46)
D. Bent	Aston Villa
J. Wilshere	Arsenal
J. Milner	Manchester City

Result 2-2   Lampard (pen), Young

2nd September 2011
v BULGARIA (ECQ)   *Sofia*

J. Hart	Manchester City
C. Smalling	Manchester United
A. Cole	Chelsea
S. Parker	Tottenham Hotspur
G. Cahill	Bolton Wanderers
J. Terry	Chelsea
T. Walcott	Arsenal (sub. A. Johnson 83)
G. Barry	Manchester City (sub. F. Lampard 80)
A. Young	Manchester Utd. (sub. J. Milner 62)
W. Rooney	Manchester United
S. Downing	Liverpool

Result 3-0   Cahill, Rooney 2

6th September 2011
v WALES (ECQ)   *Wembley*

J. Hart	Manchester City
C. Smalling	Manchester United
A. Cole	Chelsea
G. Barry	Manchester City
G. Cahill	Bolton Wanderers
J. Terry	Chelsea
S. Downing	Liverpool (sub. A. Johnson 79)
F. Lampard	Chelsea (sub. S. Parker 73)
A. Young	Manchester United
W. Rooney	Manchester Utd. (sub. A. Carroll 89)
J. Milner	Manchester City

Result 1-0   Young

7th October 2011
v MONTENEGRO (ECQ)   *Podgorica*

J. Hart	Manchester City
P. Jones	Manchester United
A. Cole	Chelsea
S. Parker	Tottenham Hotspur
G. Cahill	Bolton Wanderers
J. Terry	Chelsea
T. Walcott	Arsenal (sub. D. Welbeck 76)
G. Barry	Manchester City
D. Bent	Aston Villa (sub. F. Lampard 65)
W. Rooney	Manchester United
A. Young	Man. United (sub. S. Downing 60)

Result 2-2   Young, Bent

ENGLAND INTERNATIONAL LINE-UPS AND STATISTICS 2011-2012

12th November 2011
v SPAIN *Wembley*

J. Hart	Manchester City
J. Lescott	Manchester City
P. Jagielka	Everton
G. Johnson	Liverpool
A. Cole	Chelsea
P. Jones	Manchester Utd. (sub. J. Rodwell 57)
F. Lampard	Chelsea (sub. G. Barry 57)
J. Milner	Manchester City (sub. A. Johnson 63)
S. Parker	Tott. Hotspur (sub. K. Walker 85)
T. Walcott	Arsenal (sub. S. Downing 46)
D. Bent	Aston Villa (sub. D. Welbeck 63)

Result 1-0 Lampard

15th November 2011
v SWEDEN *Wembley*

J. Hart	Manchester City
J. Terry	Chelsea
L. Baines	Everton
G. Cahill	Bolton Wanderers
K. Walker	Tottenham Hotspur
P. Jones	Manchester United
S. Downing	Liverpool
G. Barry	Manchester City
J. Rodwell	Everton (sub. J. Milner 58)
T. Walcott	Arsenal (sub. D. Sturridge 58)
B. Zamora	Fulham (sub. D. Bent 70)

Result 1-0 Barry

29th February 2012
v NETHERLANDS *Wembley*

J. Hart	Manchester City
L. Baines	Everton
G. Cahill	Chelsea
M. Richards	Manchester City
C. Smalling	Manchester United (sub. P. Jones 64)
S. Gerrard	Liverpool (sub. D. Sturridge 33 (sub. T. Walcott 88))
A. Young	Manchester United
G. Barry	Manchester City (sub. J. Milner 46)
A. Johnson	Man. City (sub. S. Downing 61)
S. Parker	Tottenham Hotspur
D. Welbeck	Man. United (sub. F. Campbell 80)

Result 2-3 Cahill, Young

26th May 2012
v NORWAY *Oslo*

R. Green	West Ham United
P. Jagielka	Everton
L. Baines	Everton
J. Lescott	Manchester City
P. Jones	Manchester United (sub. M. Kelly 88)
S. Downing	Liverpool (sub. A. Johnson 85)
S. Gerrard	Liverpool (sub. G. Barry 46)
A. Young	Manchester United (sub. Oxlade-Chamberlain 73)
J. Milner	Manchester City
S. Parker	Tott. Hotspur (sub. T. Walcott. 56)
A. Carroll	Liverpool

Result 1-0 Young

2nd June 2012
v BELGIUM *Wembley*

J. Hart	Manchester City
A. Cole	Chelsea
J. Terry	Chelsea (sub. P. Jagielka 70)
G. Johnson	Liverpool
G. Cahill	Chelsea (sub. J. Lescott 19)
S. Gerrard	Liverpool (sub. J. Henderson 83)
A. Young	Manchester United (sub. J. Defoe 66)
J. Milner	Manchester City
S. Parker	Tottenham Hotspur
A. Oxlade-Chamberlain	Arsenal (sub. T. Walcott 67)
D. Welbeck	Manchester Utd. (sub. W. Rooney 53)

Result 1-0 Welbeck

11th June 2012
v FRANCE (EC) *Donetsk*

J. Hart	Manchester City
G. Johnson	Liverpool
A. Cole	Chelsea
S. Gerrard	Liverpool
J. Terry	Chelsea
A. Young	Manchester United
J. Lescott	Manchester City
J. Milner	Manchester City
S. Parker	Tott. Hotspur (sub. J. Henderson 78)
A. Oxlade-Chamberlain	Arsenal (sub. J. Defoe 77)
D. Welbeck	Manchester Utd. (sub. T. Walcott 90)

Result 1-1 Lescott

15th June 2012
v SWEDEN (EC)   *Kiev*

J. Hart	Manchester City
G. Johnson	Liverpool
A. Cole	Chelsea
S. Gerrard	Liverpool
J. Terry	Chelsea
A. Carroll	Liverpool
A. Young	Manchester United
J. Lescott	Manchester City
J. Milner	Manchester City (sub. T. Walcott 61)
S. Parker	Tottenham Hotspur
D. Welbeck	Manchester United (sub. A. Oxlade-Chamberlain 90)

Result 3-2   Carroll, Walcott, Welbeck

19th June 2012
v UKRAINE (EC)   *Donetsk*

J. Hart	Manchester City
G. Johnson	Liverpool
A. Cole	Chelsea
S. Gerrard	Liverpool
J. Terry	Chelsea
W. Rooney	Manchester United (sub. A. Oxlade-Chamberlain 87)
A. Young	Manchester United
J. Lescott	Manchester City
J. Milner	Manchester City (sub. T. Walcott 70)
S. Parker	Tottenham Hotspur
D. Welbeck	Manchester Utd. (sub. A. Carroll 82)

Result 1-0   Rooney

24th June 2012
v ITALY (EC)   *Kiev*

J. Hart	Manchester City
G. Johnson	Liverpool
A. Cole	Chelsea
S. Gerrard	Liverpool
J. Terry	Chelsea
W. Rooney	Manchester United
A. Young	Manchester United
J. Lescott	Manchester City
J. Milner	Manchester City (sub. T. Walcott 60)
S. Parker	Tott. Hotspur (sub. J. Henderson 94)
D. Welbeck	Manchester Utd. (sub. A. Carroll 60)

Result 0-0   AET. Italy won 4-2 on penalties

Supporters' Guides Series

This top-selling series has been published since 1982 and the new 2013 editions contain the 2011/2012 Season's results and tables, Directions, Photographs, Telephone numbers, Parking information, Admission details, Disabled information and much more.

THE SUPPORTERS' GUIDE TO PREMIER & FOOTBALL LEAGUE CLUBS 2013

This 29th edition covers all 92 Premiership and Football League clubs. *Price £7.99*

NON-LEAGUE SUPPORTERS' GUIDE AND YEARBOOK 2013

This 21st edition covers all 68 clubs in Step 1 & Step 2 of Non-League football – the Football Conference National, Conference North and Conference South. *Price £7.99*

SCOTTISH FOOTBALL SUPPORTERS' GUIDE AND YEARBOOK 2013

The 20th edition featuring all Scottish Premier League, Scottish League and Highland League clubs. *Price £7.99*

RYMAN FOOTBALL LEAGUE SUPPORTERS' GUIDE AND YEARBOOK 2012

The 2nd edition features the 66 clubs which make up the 3 divisions of the Isthmian League, sponsored by Ryman. *Price £6.99*

EVO-STIK SOUTHERN FOOTBALL LEAGUE SUPPORTERS' GUIDE AND YEARBOOK 2012

This 2nd edition features the 66 clubs which make up the 3 divisions of the Southern League, sponsored by Evo-Stik. *Price £6.99*

EVO-STIK NORTHERN PREMIER LEAGUE SUPPORTERS' GUIDE AND YEARBOOK 2012

The 2nd edition features the 67 clubs which make up the 3 divisions the Northern Premier League, sponsored by Evo-Stik. *Price £6.9*

THE SUPPORTERS' GUIDE TO WELSH FOOTBALL 2011

The enlarged 12th edition covers the 112+ clubs which make up t top 3 tiers of Welsh Football. *Price £8.99*

These books are available UK & Surface post free from –

Soccer Books Limited (Dept. SBL)
72 St. Peter's Avenue
Cleethorpes, DN35 8HU
United Kingdom